How to Conduct A Spiritual Life Retreat

How to Conduct A Spiritual Life Retreat

NORMAN SHAWCHUCK
RUEBEN P. JOB
ROBERT G. DOHERTY

The Upper Room
Nashville, Tennessee

Scripture quotations designated RSV are from the Revised Standard Version of the Bible, copyrighted 1946, 1952, and © 1971 by the Division of Christian Education, National Council of Churches of Christ in the United States of America, and are used by permission.

Scripture quotations designated NASB are from the New American Standard Bible, ©The Lockman Foundation 1960, 1962, 1963, 1968, 1971, 1972, 1973, 1975, 1977.

Scripture quotations marked NIV are from the Holy Bible, New International Version. Copyright © 1973, 1978, 1984 International Bible Society. Used by permission of Zondervan Bible Publishers.

Scripture quotations designated KJV are from the King James Version of the Bible.

Book design: Thelma Whitworth
Cover Transparency: Frances Dorris
First Printing: June 1986 (7)
Library of Congress Catalog Card Number: 85-52015
ISBN 0-8358-0527-1

Printed in the United States of America

Jesus said to them, "Come away by yourselves to a lonely place, and rest awhile."

—Mark 6:31, NASB

This life, therefore,
is not righteousness
but growth in righteousness,
not health but healing,
not being but becoming,
not rest but exercise.
We are not yet what we shall be
but we are growing toward it,
the process is not yet finished
but it is going on,
this is not the end
but it is the road.
All does not yet gleam in glory
but all is being purified.

—Martin Luther

Contents

Preface

O God, thou art my God, I shall seek Thee earnestly;
My soul thirsts for Thee, as a body wasted with longing
for Thee—like a dry and thirsty land that has no water.

—Psalm 63:1, NASB

It is intense longing, a deep thirsting for God, which draws us to enter into retreat—whether for a few moments alone in the closets of our hearts (Matt. 6:6) or for an extended period of time in an isolated place (Luke 9:28; Mark 6:46).

The thirsty soul retreats from pressing responsibilities and frenzied schedules for a few moments, or for several hours, in order to pray. Both in retreat moments and in the prayer offered, there is reason to love God; for it is God's love that draws us to retreat, and love is the fruit of our prayers.

If you ever marvel at a tree laden with fruit and wonder about the secret of its fruitfulness, you soon begin considering the connection between the tree and its branches and the tree and the fertile soil which hides the tree's roots, holding the entire tree seurely in its place. We can compare the life of the fruitful Christian with the fruit-laden tree. There is no fruitful life apart from a lively connection with Christ or apart from solid roots in a fertile "inner room" of prayer. This inner room provides us the necessary nutrition to sustain our deepest inner selves—a "life hidden with Christ in God" (Col. 3:3; *see also* Matt. 6:6; John 15:1-16).

And the greatest marvel of all is that such a life is fruitful without strain or worry. The tree itself did nothing to bear such a rich harvest of fruit. Just a few weeks ago it shivered, cold and lonely, in the winter. On the surface it seemed surely dead, never to bear fruit again. But the warm sun came to melt the snow and kiss the cold, frozen ground. A soft breeze gently shook the tree awake just in time to hear the song of a joyful bird. When the conditions were right a little flower appeared, and then its fruit.

So it is with the child of God. When the conditions are right we *will* bear fruit—for Christ has chosen us to bear fruit and has promised that our fruit will last (John 15:16). The conditions are made right in us when we develop the habit of retreating to be with God in meditation and prayer and then moving back into the world to give incarnational expression to the Word God has spoken to us there.

We have a wonderful illustration of the power of prayer and retreat to transform our entire being and to put us in conversation with God in order that we may bear rich fruit (Mark

9:20-29; Luke 9:28-34). But until we "wake up" to the power of prayer to transform our lives we will, like the three friends of Jesus, choose to sleep instead of pray. We succumb to the trivia of the daily grind rather than retreat to the "mountain" alone with Christ.

In *Merton's Palace of Nowhere*, James Finley shares some important advice he received from Thomas Merton:

> Merton once told me to quit trying so hard in prayer. He said: "How does an apple ripen? It just sits in the sun." A small green apple cannot ripen in one night by tightening all its muscles, squinting its eyes and tightening its jaw in order to find itself the next morning miraculously large, red, ripe, and juicy beside its small green counterparts. Like the birth of a baby or the opening of a rose, the birth of the true self takes place in God's time. We must wait for God, we must be awake; we must trust in his hidden action within us.

By now you have probably noticed that we are referring to retreats in two ways. One of those is a daily time when we withdraw into ourselves for a brief conversation with God. The other is that more infrequent opportunity to withdraw to a more isolated place for an extended season of prayer, reflection, and serious Christian conversation.

This book is primarily concerned with retreats to a more solitary place where the longing soul may spend a few days in unhurried conversation with God and other pilgrims. We send this book forth in hope that it may provide you the same blessed opportunity in God's presence which we experience in such retreats—and which we observe revivifying the lives of many who have journeyed away with us on retreat.

In another book we have provided a complete set of helps to guide your daily retreats.[1] It has already made its way around the world to become a daily companion of thousands who thirst for God. We commend it to you for your daily use, even as we do this book to further instruct you in the spiritual life and to assist you in planning and conducting retreats for others.

And now we leave you in the hands of the Holy Spirit to guide your journey—often in the desert, sometimes upon the mountain—but always in the care of Christ, who loves you and waits for you in a place apart.

NORMAN SHAWCHUCK

Part 1

An Overview of the Spiritual Life

1.

Wandering toward the Promised Land

A WANDERING JOURNEY

We would all like to think that our spiritual growth and maturity might proceed something like this:

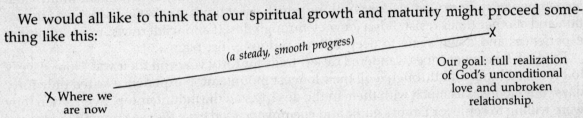

(a steady, smooth progress)

X Where we
are now

Our goal: full realization
of God's unconditional
love and unbroken
relationship.

Most of us, however, do not experience our journey toward God this way. As a second choice we would gladly settle for a Christian growth experience that would go something like this:

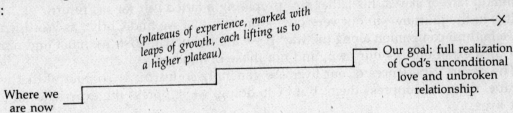

*(plateaus of experience, marked with
leaps of growth, each lifting us to
a higher plateau)*

Where we
are now

Our goal: full realization
of God's unconditional
love and unbroken
relationship.

But most of us do not experience spiritual growth like this either.

A map in the back of one of our Bibles depicts the journey of the Israelites from slavery in Egypt to the promised land something like this:

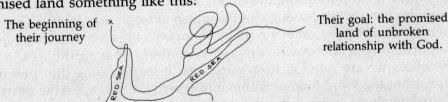

The beginning of
their journey

Their goal: the promised
land of unbroken
relationship with God.

God's children have always experienced the faithful life as a journey, a wandering, toward the promised land. The entire Old Testament is set in the context of God's children on a wandering journey. Adam and Eve begin the journey by wandering away from the paradise God desires for them. The journey is taken up by their descendants, who after many generations wander into Egypt and slavery.

After many more generations they journey out of Egypt, across the Red Sea, through the wilderness (a journey of days that took them forty years), to the Promised Land. At long last Adam's children have come home. The journey has gone full cycle from the Garden of Eden to the Promised Land.

And so it is with us. Born into the possibility of living all our days at "home" with God, it isn't long until we take our own journey into a foreign land where we spend all the provisions God has so generously given us. It isn't until we find ourselves starving for our "daily bread" that we decide to begin the journey back home. And so we return—tired, guilt-ridden, hungry, fearful, willing to settle for slavery as long as we get enough food to keep us alive. Then, to our great surprise, we discover that God is waiting with robe, ring, shoes, and a superabundance of food.

When Jesus told the story of the prodigal son and his elder brother (Luke 15:11-32), he compressed the entire Old Testament story into the experience of these two brothers. And in so doing, he also told us about the journey we make. We have met the brothers and they are us!

The spiritual life and the process of spiritual formation is much more a journey than a condition or a "place" where we can settle down. It is a journey sometimes toward God, sometimes away from God, a journey along which we at times accept God's love and invitation and at other times resist. It is a journey through desert and wilderness, to mountaintop experiences and down again to deep valleys and long, flat plains.

The Old Testament tribes wandered desert trails for forty years on their way from slavery to promised land, and through it all their longest mountaintop experience lasted only forty days. But God was as much with them in the desert as on the mountaintop. Even when they were willing to settle for Egypt's garlic and cucumbers, God gave them a superabundance of angel's food.

The prodigal son learned about such things. Even as he was preparing to settle for the common fare of slaves, his father was preparing a fatted calf for his return.

It is in the journey—in our very own journey—that we find Christ, as Word, coming to us, a faithful companion along the way. If we are to know Christ, we must find him within our own experiences—our own, and not those of another.

The desert experiences of our lives are generally so fearful or so painful that we try to escape, deny, or suppress them. But in so doing, we suppress the experience of Christ in our lives.

We flock like starving souls to find the food we crave in the experience of another—converted movie stars, sports heroes, notorious criminals, or perhaps even bishops. But their experience cannot be our own food, and so we go away a bit jealous that God has been so good to them while leaving us to languish alone in our desert.

In order to discover God in the affairs of our own lives, we must not deny, seek to escape, or suppress any of life's experiences as they confront us along the way. In running from our experiences we are running from ourselves. In suppressing the "desert" within, we are suppressing the Word hidden within our experience and speaking to us from there.

Somehow those colorful, generally rebellious, often-in-trouble folk of the Old Testament discovered this early in their own lives. For that reason they spent much time reflecting upon their own experience, telling their story over and over again, taking great care to insure that the story would be told to their children and their children's children. It was in reflecting upon and rehearsing their own story that they found God present and adequate for their present circumstance. Such reflection and rehearsal revived their faith, helped them discover answers to problems, and gave them courage to confront their most formidable enemies.

It is important to notice that the Old and New Testament biblical heroes give witness to the fact that this process of reflecting and telling one's life story cannot be done alone. In support of this, Dietrich Bonhoeffer in *Life Together*[1] said, "The Christian needs another Christian who speaks God's Word to him. . . . The Christ in his own heart is weaker than the Christ in the word of his brother; his own heart is uncertain, his brother's is sure."

Such serious conversation requires time and a place set apart—a covenant community meeting regularly or a spiritual retreat where persons gather to reflect upon and discuss the movements of God in their lives.

KNOWING OURSELVES AND BEING ONE WITH GOD

Whether regularly in a small group meeting or in a retreat setting where persons may be together but once, there are six attitudes which can assist us in remaining more sensitive to the Word, which is seeking to make itself known through our life experiences. These attitudes, described on the following pages, open us to the Spirit, the inner Voice, which calls to us from within.

1. *Praying with mind and heart together.* One of the most vital elements of the spiritual life is the ability to "pray with the heart." That which fills and satisfies the soul is not so much head knowledge as it is a felt understanding and a relishing of things in our interior selves.

The desert fathers taught their disciples to pray, standing before God "with the mind in the heart." What is being sought here is the involvement of the whole person in prayer; that is, being fully real before the real God, alive with all the inner and outer motions and commotions that make up the "enfleshed spirit" that we are—a physical body, human feelings and emotions, rational mind, and deep intuitions. This prayer of the whole person is affective prayer, or "prayer with the heart."

Without such affective prayer, the self-awareness that is so necessary for spiritual growth will remain underdeveloped. And without growing self-awareness there can be little personal experience of spiritual consolation or desolation, no contrasting action and reaction of the "spirits," all of which are necessary to Christian discernment of the Word of God to our lives.

There are many resources for enabling persons to enter into prayer with affectivity, such as: meditating upon scripture or other devotional writings, fasting, journaling, participating in the Lord's Supper and worship, and doing acts of mercy.

2. *Reflecting upon life's experiences.* This takes us a step further into the contemplative process by drawing us beyond merely feeling experience to relooking at experience as it is happening to us, and then integrating experience into our consciousness.

Few people really seek to incorporate their experience into their consciousness. Rather, they try to suppress the painful experience quickly and to escape the dull monotony of the daily grind by projecting themselves into a fantasized future of even greater pain or ectasy.

In Thornton Wilder's play *Our Town*, Emily asks whether people ever live life while they have it every day. The stage manager insists that, except for some poets and saints, persons do not live life while they have it.

So it is that few of us ever discover who we are, and therefore can never know who God is for us, because we do not relook at our life experiences in order to integrate their lessons and revelations into our own consciousness.

3. *Articulating or giving witness to our experience.* The growth process, psychological and spiritual, is predicated upon the need to communicate one's innermost movements, feelings, and thoughts to another. This is the means by which we bring objectivity to our subjectivity.

To articulate our experience gives it a greater sense of realness and allows us to relive it in leisure.

The process of entrusting another with our "story" makes us transparent before God and is of itself one of the most affective means of prayer, opening us to the possibility of new revelations of the Word for our lives. Indeed, the psalmist demonstrates how the witness of his own experience, whether dark wrestlings or joyous celebrations, leads to revelation (see Ps. 145).

4. *Spiritually discerning the Word of God as it is speaking in and through our experience.* This is the growing ability which flows from and makes use of all that has been said above. Reflection upon and articulation of experience begins by being merely descriptive and ends by being interpretative. This is the art, science, and charism of spiritual discernment.

Discernment is essentially the task of the person at prayer, but it is also a cooperative venture in and through dialogue as believing persons clarify issues together, sometimes praying together, always asking God's light and guidance so that they might interpret the deeper meaning of their inner and outer experiences.

Once the deeper meaning of life's experiences has been discovered, the process of discernment enables the individual or group to experience God as an active participant in decisions which may emerge regarding present and future action as response to the Word spoken through experience.

5. *Sustaining times of solitude.* Perhaps the single most significant element in spiritual experience, the backdrop to all forms of prayer, is solitude. Most authors list "silence of the heart," inner space and outer stillness, as the most important climate for a relational spirituality.

Solitude and silence are the essential conditions that favor deep retrieval for personal integration of all facets of the human-divine relationship. A supportive, praying community is the preferable context out of which we enter into the desert of solitude. The boundaries surrounding one's desert of solitude are the love of an intimate community.[2] This leads to the sixth and the final element essential for spiritual growth.

6. *Entering into covenantal community relationships.* Jesus recognized the need for such relationships and began his ministry by entering into intimate community with twelve persons. Further, he invited an even more intimate group of three persons to support him in his experiences of extreme agony (in the garden) and of extreme ecstasy (on the Mount of Transfiguration) and to bolster his faith (Luke 8:51-55).

John Wesley discovered times of solitude and times of community to be essential for himself and his contemporaries. Thus he laid equal emphasis upon daily times of solitude for personal reflection and private prayer and upon meeting regularly with a small group for serious Christian conversation.

The necessity of a community to sustain one's journey into solitude becomes clear when we consider the double meaning of the "desert" as a biblical symbol:

• Scriptures portray the desert as the privileged meeting place of God.

• Scriptures also portray the desert as the dwelling place of evil spirits, the place where "testing" of Christian values goes on, where the person at prayer enters into struggle and darkness at all levels of the heart. Wrestling with the darkness in our own heart is often a fearful experience, made possible only in the awareness that a community attends us (Mark 1:13).

SUMMARY

In this chapter we have said that growth in the spiritual life is often experienced as a wandering journey. We have also said that there are basic attitudes which give us a discerning heart to reflect upon life experiences in order to discover the Lord as faithful companion along the way.

There is hardly a more opportune setting in which we can develop or strengthen these attitudes than a spiritual life retreat. In a retreat we may begin to pray with the heart, find unhurried moments to reflect upon the deeper movements in our lives, and enter into the serious Christian dialogue which so often provides the light and inspiration needed to make ourselves real before God and to receive God's Word in response to our realness.

A retreat can be designed to allow as much time for solitude and for Christian community as is helpful to the retreatant's particular stage on his/her journey. When this is happening under the sensitive care of a retreat leader who knows how to listen to another's story, and to provide persons the space they need to make themselves real before the Lord, something good is certain to happen!

2.

The Pathways to Growth in the Spiritual Life

There is no fixed formula by which God seeks to enter our lives. God comes to us through an almost infinite variety of experiences and refuses to prescribe the manner by which we grow in grace. However, God does have one ultimate goal for us all—a "oneing" of our mind, spirit, and body with God. Becoming one with God is already prefigured in our baptismal union with Jesus Christ. We finally perceive this "oneing" that God has been about all along in prevenient grace and through the sacrament of baptism.

Having once gained an entry through the circumstances of our life, the Lord of life, through the indwelling presence of the Spirit, leads the sensitive and believing Christian along the path of spiritual maturity. Through the "ups and downs," times of darkness and light, the struggles to be free, the abiding joy of friendships and love, the pain of loss and failure, the unexpected blessings and the unprepared deaths—through all of these human happenings—the Holy Spirit is constant companion and guide if only we open ourselves to the Spirit's sure leading.

Sometimes the progress in guidance is direct; at other times it is indirect and less obvious. Sometimes we remain at one level of growth for a period of time, seemingly static and unmoving; at other times we are led along on a clearly advancing path, challenged by newness and faced with very little human resistance to God's direction for our lives. Sometimes we double back to struggle with a matter again and again. At other times we lay the matter to rest through complete acceptance of God's will regarding the matter; there is no need for us to pass this way again.

The invitation to a deeper intimacy with God is always being offered, but our state of readiness can be quite superficial. With patience and good will, however, we can grow beyond our fondest expectations. In spite of (or perhaps because of) our wanderings the journey is leading us nearer our goal. In *That Man Is You*, Louis Evely says, "Abraham started out not knowing where he was going, and that was a sure sign he was going in the right direction."

Over the years we have listened attentively to the life stories our retreatants have had to tell, and we have paid close attention to those experiences which they described as moments of new insight or breakthroughs into greater awareness of the presence of God, and God's will for their lives. Through all our listening we have constantly been searching to understand how persons enter into a conscious relationship with God and how they nurture that relationship so that it remains constant and vital. We have discovered that God's leading is intentional—God is leading each one of us somewhere. These discoveries are neither new nor novel; they simply parallel the observations of other spiritual guides, both ancient and modern.[1]

While each person's life history is unique, nevertheless each one of us sooner or later, perhaps many times, is drawn by the Spirit to travel certain pathways of spiritual growth. Being aware of this, we as spiritual guides can accompany others in ways that will facilitate their progress along the pathway.

As a resource to your own spiritual growth and your work with others, we will present the pathways which it seems all of us must travel on our way to spiritual maturity. As you study the outline, please remember that the process of spiritual growth is not a ladderlike set of stages. Rather it is a back-and-forth, rhythmic pattern, sometimes advancing, sometimes regressing. The divine initiative is ever acting; the human resistance always possible. Breakthrough into new spiritual growth comes as the individual or the community responds to grace and thereby journeys a little farther into the kingdom of God.

It is important to recognize that these pathways are not sequential or parallel. Rather, they are more of a helix, an intertwined set of experiences that are each interrelated and influenced by the others. At the same time each is distinct from the others so that from time to time each one is lifted up by the Spirit for our review and response.

We will from time to time travel along each of the pathways in our journey toward that "oneing" God desires with all of us. Put another way, each pathway may become the point through which God finds entrance into our conscious selves. Christ is always knocking at the door which he believes we can open easily to him at a particular time: "Behold, I stand at the door and knock; if anyone hears My voice and opens the door, I will come in to eat with him and him with Me" (Rev. 3:20, NASB).

Having once found a point of openness in our lives, however, he will immediately set to work reconstructing and rearranging us; we will experience this construction as growth along the pathways. These pathways are:

Conversion: the process, based upon a bedrock assurance of God's love for us, that leads us to take a thorough inventory of ourselves and gradually to surrender up to God's forgiveness all that we discover which separates us from God.

Service: a conscious or subconscious response to a call to make the world a better place for all of God's creatures, to push back moral darkness in any guise so that the kingdom of God may occupy larger territory. This service may be offered in the arena of our daily lives as we go about our occupation or volunteer work and as we relate to those around us.

Passion: a commitment to serve God to the extent that we become willing to endure hardship, suffering, and even death in order to help the vision of a better world become reality. The willingness to stand in another's place in times of suffering or oppression, the grace to view our own suffering (illness, poverty, rejection, grief) as filling up the cup of Christ's redemptive suffering for the world. We suffer that he need not suffer so much; we weep that he need not weep alone.

Union with Christ: the conscious realization that the sacramental union of Baptism and Holy Communion is becoming a union of will and action. We have been drawn into a greater maturity in Christ; thus, we grow a little nearer to God. We have gone a few steps farther into kingdom living and toward a new realization of God's love for us.

Each of these pathways is God's entry point into our lives. On these pathways we journey toward greater spiritual maturity and intimacy. We do not make the journey to full maturity all in one step along any of these pathways, and herein lies a paradox: having once repented, having let go of our sins and invited Christ into our "territory," we are converted. At that moment we are as much a child of God, living in God's salvation, as we will ever be; but there are still areas of our lives that are not yet converted. We are still being transformed through the process of discovering God's complete will for our lives (Rom. 12:1–2); and this process will go on until the day we finally see God.

In the meantime as we journey along, we continue to make discoveries about parts of ourselves that we have not yet surrendered up to God's will. We are already converted, but we are still being converted more and more into God's likeness.

How do we discover these territories within that are not yet surrendered up to God? By journeying along the pathways of service, passion, and union. Along the way we discover that while we are willing to serve God in *this* we are not yet willing to serve God in *that*; that while we are willing to give our lives to Christian service for God's kingdom, we are not yet willing to leave friends and family and live in poverty in order to serve God among the people on the fringes of society. We discover that while we are willing to attend church every Sunday, sing in the choir, and even give large sums to help feed the poor, we are not yet willing to begin getting up daily at 5 A.M. in order to spend an unhurried hour in intimate communion with God.

At each discovery point we are confronted with the need to decide. Shall we surrender this newly discovered territory to God, thus allowing this area of our lives to be converted, transformed; or shall we say, "No, God, I am converted enough. I will not let go of this piece of territory—at least not yet."

And so it is that the pathways intertwine in our experience. God will enter our lives wherever there is acceptance and will continue the process of moving into our territory at the point of greatest vulnerability and/or readiness.

But while God enters any open pathway, there is a progression in spiritual maturity. The journey is to lead us somewhere. God has definite growth goals in mind for us. Paul is clear about that when he says: "By this time you should be teachers, but you still have need for someone to teach you the elementary principles of the Christian life. You are still not able to eat solid food. You still need milk. Milk is for babies, but solid food is for the mature (Heb. 5:12–14, AP). And so like children of Israel, we wander the pathways, but what seems like wandering to us is purposeful to God. This journey is taking us somewhere.

We will now proceed to cast the pathways into a format which may be helpful to you as you seek to companion persons, to guide them in reflection and dialogue which may facilitate their growth along these dimensions.

Conversion: the unfailing love of God draws us from sin to salvation, darkness into light, unfreedom to freedom

The Divine Initiative. *God sends Jesus to us in love (1 John 4:9-10).* The basic foundation for all spiritual growth is God's loving gift of Jesus. Through God's promises and initiatives, God assures us that we are already loved just as we are. We don't have to go anywhere or do anything to gain God's love. This love is unconditional and unmerited. To fall into the hands of God is to fall into the arms of unfailing love (Mic. 7:18–19).

There is a divine initiative in our every encounter with God. Even before we knew our Creator, God loved us. Even before we turned to look toward God, God was moving toward us.

Our faintest yearning for God is assurance that God is already longing for us. Our first feeble step toward God is possible only because God has already been moving toward us, drawing us nearer by the divine magnet-heart of love. It is quite common, however, for the Christian to lose the experiential realization of God's longing for us. While we may hold to it intellectually, the actual experience of it may grow dim, or be lost altogether.

The Human Response. *We open ourselves to the sign of God's love (Ps. 139:23–24).* The realization of God's love for us comes as a life–changing, liberating moment. Jesus announced his ministry as one of setting persons free from the effects of sin and darkness to enjoy a life of complete freedom and full salvation.

The "inhabitants" of the dark recesses of our conscious and subconscious selves are often so fear–or guilt–producing that we go to almost any length to avoid admitting or confronting their existence. But once the realization of God's unconditional love is secure, we begin to look into the dark side of life's experiences in order to be led from that darkness into the light (Col. 1:13–14). God's love for us means we need not stay as we are, for the Holy Spirit is with us to help us face ourselves and to go from where we are to where God wants us to be.

Conversion is a journey. The Christian *is* saved and *is being* saved. Just as the child is not fully mature, so the Christian is not fully mature at the time of "birth" in Christ. As the Christian grows, the Spirit reveals attitudes and behaviors which frustrate the search for wholeness. For this reason the Christian will be aware of the conflict between resistance and acceptance of the will of God, between darkness and light.

As we grow in Christ, we will develop sensibilities which detect the slightest imperfection in desire or deed grievous to the Spirit. This growth process is experienced as an interior struggle between the kingdom of God and the kingdom of darkness (Rom. 7:14–25). It is important in the struggle to experience God's unconditional love as a foundation to stand on while reviewing our lives and moving from unfreedom into freedom (Rom. 8:1-14).

The Letting Go. There is a necessary *metanoia* in each breakthrough into further spiritual growth, a necessary change of heart which will lead to a new conversion of one's attitudes and behaviors. There must be a "letting go" of something in our lives in order to make room for the "laying hold" of a new and higher consciousness of the presence and claims of God.

At this point the necessary change of heart is to become willing to accept the wonder that God already loves us just as we are and to surrender to the consequences of that love—both to God and to ourselves.

God's love flows like a river into our life situations and, like a river, its benefits can be dammed up behind the human tendency to resist unconditional love and the very idea that we are lovable.

The change of heart at this stage involves a willingness to let go of the very things which cause us most hurt—our sin and the psychic prisons in which we have locked away our most cherished dreams, potentialities, and spontaneities, as well as the darkness that causes us to stumble in our efforts toward new dimensions in life.

We cling to our resistances simply because it seems too good to be true that we are being invited through God's love to surrender our sin for salvation, our prisons for freedom, and our darkness for light. But when we are able finally to break through our resistance we find ourselves in a new dimension of life and relationship (John 10:10).

Scriptures for meditation to assist persons dealing with this faith issue are: Deut.

30:11–31:8; Pss. 8; 139; 13:5–6; 23; Isa. 43:1–7; Ezek. 36:25–28; Mic. 7:18–19; Luke 7:36–50; 15:11–32; 19:1–10; John 3:16; 8:1–11; Rom. 6:28–39; Eph. 4:22–24; 1 John 4:9–10.

Service: Christ calls us to join him in the struggle between the kingdom of God and the kingdom of darkness.

The Divine Initiative. *Christ reveals to us as much of his own kingdom vision as we are able to bear.* Whenever we take a step toward Christ, he responds in a way that tells us the step did not go unnoticed. His response is always designed to give us further insight into the nature of the kingdom of God and our place in it. It is as though Jesus were saying, "Now that you have turned my way, I want to share with you something of my vision of how good life can be for you, and for all creation, as you journey farther into the kingdom of God."

Our letting go of former attitudes and behaviors has made it possible for Christ to create within us a new consciousness of the kingdom of God and its rightful claim upon our lives. Jesus does this by setting up a situation in which we must again decide our response to him. The situation may seem almost trivial, but the consequences of our response will prove to have life-altering effects. For example, how might Zacchaeus's life been different had he not come down out of his tree, as Jesus commanded (Luke 19:5)? Or what would we know of Peter today had he refused to loan Jesus his boat (Luke 5:3)?

The Human Response. *We answer the call to service.* The steps we have taken in response to God's love have taken a niche out of the unconquered territory within, and now the kingdom of God advances to occupy that territory. There comes a new realization of what Jesus meant when he said, "The kingdom of God is within you" (Luke 17:21, RSV).

As we mature in faith God makes increasing demands upon our time, resources, and energies. We are being challenged to join with God in making the divine vision come true for all the world around us.

The Letting Go. The resistance experienced here is born of a fear that Christ will ask too much, the cost of service will be too great, or the demands may outstrip our capacities— "What if I risk and fail?"

The Christian must now let go of the notion of "cheap grace" (wanting to have Christ as Savior only, but not as Sovereign Lord of all of one's life), to lay hold of the fact that we are called to a life of full maturity, obedience, and service (Heb. 6:1-2; Titus 3:14).

Scriptures for meditation along this pathway are: Matt. 4:18-22; Mark 4:26-41; 6:30-34; Luke 5:1-10; 9:23-26; 10:1-16; 18:18-30; John 1:29-34; 8:31-51; 10:1-30; 15:1-7; 21:1-11; Gal. 5:16-25; Eph. 6:10-20; Phil. 3:7-14; James 3:13-18.

Passion: The cost of discipleship. Jesus invites us to enter into the deeper mysteries of his passion, the paschal suffering.

The Divine Initiative. *Jesus shows us that the fruits of our labor are born only in the crucible of suffering (John 12:24).* To those who engage in his service, Jesus extends the invitation, sooner or later, to share also in his suffering. There is a certain glory in sharing his service, but an ignominy in sharing his suffering, given the values of our world.

The Human Response. Encounter with this faith issue proves to be a "watershed" experience for many Christians who are willing to serve but unwilling to enter into the pain, passion, and suffering required for further spiritual growth (Mark 10:17-22). The resistance experienced here is the human urge to back away from pain and self–abandonment or the very idea that we may suffer in Christ's stead.

Service in the kingdom comes at a price. Discipleship has its cost. Many of us resist, fearing the cost. Perhaps more of us resist because we do not believe Christ needs us—"The idea that I can do anything significant to advance God's purposes is a dream, an impossible dream."

The Letting Go. The breakthrough comes as we realize that we are chosen and appointed by God to a unique and important ministry in the divine kingdom and that the fruits of this ministry are germinated and multiplied in the crucible of suffering (John 12:24-28).

Breakthrough comes as we are given the grace to entrust ourselves to the paschal mystery. As we move into this mystery we make two rather startling discoveries. We discover a deeper, more vital fellowship with Christ in sharing his sufferings (Phil. 4:10), and we discover that the passion experience produces a deep and profound joy and satisfaction, not sorrow or despair (Heb. 12:2).

The decision to surrender everything, to endure all things, and to continue companionship with Christ gives us a discerning heart, not only into our own situation but also into the situation of others. Having struggled with our own choices, we are now able to identify with the struggles of others. Gone is the tendency to criticize and judge. In its place has come a generous love and concern. Now, and only now, can we engage in intercessory prayer borne on the wings of perfect love. Such prayer is with power because the person praying is much more sensitive to discern the situation the other is facing.

Intercessory prayer is much more than words; it is standing in another's stead, even to the point of death. Such prayer often requires life and death choices, for to enter into Christ's passion requires that we respond to others around us with the same quality of unconditional love that God has for us. For this reason several of the church fathers refer to this stage of spiritual growth as "contemplation to attain perfect love."

Scriptures for meditation along this pathway are: Pss. 35; 55; 113-118; Matt. 26:57-68; Mark 8:34-38; Luke 14:25-35; 22:7-23, 39-46; 23:26-32, 33-46; John 12:23-33; 13:1-6; 14:7-19; 19:17-37.

Union with Christ: The journey leads to an ever closer identity and relationship with Christ.

The Divine Initiative. *Jesus draws us into closer union with himself through incarnation and resurrection.* The ultimate goal Christ holds for us is that we become his bride without infidelity, that we enter into a love relationship free of all mixed motives, desires, or behavior. He is ever pursuing us, courting us, calling us into such union with him. This mystery, says Paul, is profound (Eph. 5:32, RSV).

In his attempt to describe the relationship which Christ so deeply yearns to have with us, Paul draws comparisons with the physio-spiritual union that grows between a man and a woman who give themselves completely, without reservation, to each other (Eph. 5:22-32). Unfortunately this passage is usually read as Paul's teaching regarding relationships in marriage, but Paul's primary focus was upon our relationship with Christ—"I am speaking with references to Christ and the church" (v. 32, NASB).

This passage provides poignant insight into the deep desire of Christ to take us as his very own. He wants us to leave father and mother; that is, to surrender other primary relationships in order to become one flesh with him (v. 31). He wants us to be his alone, with no spot or blame; and in love he provides for this through his own sacrifice (vv. 25-27).

As we labor, suffer, and serve with Christ, we grow closer to him, more like him. We experience "oneing" through the integration of motives and behaviors. We come finally to understand that he wants to be with us forever in a most intimate relationship. He wants to interpenetrate our body with his body, our mind and spirit with his own, so that we may truly become bone of his bone and flesh of his flesh. He moves ever closer to us, until there comes a union of his spirit and energy with our own. Not only does he join his life with ours, he also enables us to rise above all the obstacles and limitations which frustrate our journey toward him (John 11:25, 43-44; Heb. 6:1).

The Human Response. When we seek to be like Christ we come to realize that we are facing an eternal paradox—the more we become like him the greater is our realization that we are not yet fully like him. This growing similarity makes us more conscious of the vast dissimilarity. But there is increased faith that he will never stop drawing us until we are fully formed in the image and likeness of God. He is ever moving toward us with transformation as the goal (Rom. 12:1-2).

The realization of transformation brings with it two crisis-laden insights. The first regards our resistance to enter into full personhood. Jesus is much more than savior. He is Lord. Many persons are willing to have Christ as savior. Far fewer are willing to surrender everything they possess and desire to his Lordship. But union with Christ makes this possible: all that we have is already his—and all he has is already ours. It is a small, albeit momentarily painful, sacrifice to surrender what we fleetingly possess in order to make room for all he is desiring to share with us forever.

The second insight regards the fullness of Christ's mission. Union with Christ means we will share not only his glory but also his passion and suffering. He invites us not only to live with him but also to die with him (Mark 8:34-38). The mystery here reminds us that Christ yet suffers for the redemption of God's creation, and we can share his suffering. Because of us he need no longer be alone in the garden of suffering. We can shed his tears and bear his stripes.

These two insights—that we must accept Jesus as Lord as well as savior and that we must share his suffering as well as his glory—introduce much tension into our relationship with Christ. We only now begin to understand what transformation fully entails. We must now make critical choices, choices of a vastly different type than those previously made. The choices between light and darkness are always made between a good and a bad thing. The choices which must now be made, however, are always between two apparent goods—one a deceptive good and the other a real good. But on the surface, both appear to be good and valid choices.

Standard decision-making methods will no longer suffice. Only the grace to discern the mind of God will do, for we have now been given an invitation to identify with Christ at the deepest level, and the choice between two goods actually involves a decision to remain in union with Christ or to begin to turn away from Christ.

Here the Christian experiences much ambiguity regarding the will of God, because it is a basic human tendency to strongly resist any relationship or circumstance that calls for total surrender. Furthermore, there is often the tendency to resist the idea that we are so lovable and of such character that God should desire to "one" himself with us through Christ or that our companionship is so pleasant that God should yearn to be with us forever.

The Letting Go. The breakthrough into more intimate union with Christ comes as we are given the grace to find the Risen Lord already present in all the events of our lives, and so come to realize that full transformation is not a future experience only. Indeed, Christ has been drawing us into such relationship from the first moment we began to journey with him.

Electing to give Christ complete ownership of our life and to enter into union with him releases a flood of new life possibilities. There is a constant renewing of life with unlimited potential and consequence as we realize and act upon the truth that resurrection is a present reality in the spiritual life. If ever we are to be immortal, we are immortal now. There is a quality of Christian living which makes this not merely a proposition, but an experiential possibility.

Scriptures for meditation along this pathway are: Pss. 62; 136; 139; Isa. 30:18-26; 35:1-10; Mark 16:1-8; Luke 20:27-39; 24:13-35; John 3:36; 11:1-44; 20:11-29; Rom. 12:1-21; 1 Cor. 6:15; 15:1-58; 2 Cor. 11:2; Eph. 1:1-14; Phil. 2:1-15; Col. 3:12-17; 1 John 1:1-4.

SUMMARY

In this chapter we have described one model for viewing and facilitating spiritual growth. While it is helpful to have some such model in mind as you design and conduct spiritual life retreats, your model need not be the one discussed in this chapter. Whatever your model, however, it must be faithful to the biblical witness and attested to by the spiritual divines of the church.

The Gospel of Mark is constructed to lead the reader through a step-by-step consideration of the basic faith issues. For this reason a prayerful reading of the Gospel will almost certainly lead the reader into a serious consideration of his or her own journey. We have prepared a simple diagram of Mark's gospel which we sometimes use with persons desiring a private retreat (see pp. 106–7).

We will devote Part 2 of this book to designing and conducting spiritual life retreats. In the materials which follow you will have little difficulty observing how we incorporate the six elements necessary for assisting us to know ourselves and remain open to God's grace. You will also see how we allow our understanding of the pathways to spiritual maturity to inform our process designs for retreat settings.

Part 2

Tools for Designing and Conducting Spiritual Life Retreats

Introduction to Part 2
WHAT IS A SPIRITUAL LIFE RETREAT?
WHY SUCH AN INTEREST IN THEM TODAY?

This section provides resources for persons who want to plan or conduct spiritual life retreats. We have decided to share some of our retreat models with you because many people are wanting something more in their lives, an extra ingredient to supply a zest and a community often lacking in our impersonal, technological society.

The Spirit is using this hunger as an opportunity to draw us back into our interior selves, to examine the vitality and validity of our faith. This journey inward to reflect upon our deeper values and commitments will be enhanced by:

• A friend with some experience to point the way, to suggest methods and resources, to walk along as pilgrim companion.

• Unhurried periods of solitude and silence to "listen" to our own experience and thus to become acquainted with ourselves and God at deeper levels.

• One or more persons with whom to engage in serious Christian conversation in order to discern the movements of God within.

Spiritual life retreat offers opportunities for these in a manner perhaps not available to most Christians in any other setting. For this reason spiritual life retreats are becoming increasingly more popular among persons of all ages.

Our own work in conducting retreats leaves us with more invitations than we can accept. In an effort to meet this demand more adequately, we have trained and encouraged others—both lay and clergy—to offer themselves to this needed and satisfying ministry. The experiences of these persons have given us the courage to make available to you a number of our retreat models as a possible means of encouraging you to this good work.

The first requirement for your success is that you be on your own faith journey with Christ. The Spirit is not recruiting spectators, but participants, persons who will not merely point the way, but will be going there themselves. The successful retreat is always a real journey in companionship.

The second requirement is that you know enough about group dynamics to have some confidence in your ability to lead a group through the process, and that you have enough knowledge about basic patterns of listening to help another grow through serious conversation.

Spiritual life retreats come in many shapes and sizes, each designed to respond most effectively to where the retreatants are in their own faith journey. Each retreat design must take into account the constraints of time, space, and number of retreatants. This section will give designs for several types of retreats—dialogical, personally guided, preached, and private. We will begin with a brief definition of each and then proceed to give more detailed information and designs.

TYPES OF RETREATS

THE DIALOGICAL RETREAT. The dialogical retreat relies heavily on dialogue (serious Christian conversation) in small groups. The small group discussions are supported by brief lectures and times of private reflection.

The dialogical retreat is perhaps the best place for retreatants and retreat leaders to begin. It is a good beginning for the retreatant, since it provides shorter periods of solitude and longer periods of discussion. Long periods of silence and solitude are often difficult for the beginning retreatant, while group discussion is a much more familiar activity.

For the leader, the dialogical retreat requires less by way of content and somewhat less need to be in touch with what is going on in each retreatant's inner self.

THE PERSONALLY GUIDED RETREAT. The personally guided retreat involves content lectures by the guide. These lectures are planned to assist the retreatant's reflection. In this type of retreat there are relatively long periods of solitude and silence to reflect, read, and pray, as well as opportunities for each retreatant to meet privately with the guide to discuss what is happening during the times of silent reflection.

Because substantial time is given for individuals to meet privately with the guide, one guide can accommodate perhaps no more than six retreatants. Larger numbers of retreatants will require additional guides.

As persons become more comfortable with silence and interior reflection, they will find themselves desiring the extended solitude a personally guided retreat can afford. In our experience, this happens after a person has participated in two or three dialogical retreats and has developed some regular prayer disciplines. One in-depth experience seems to lead to the other.

THE PREACHED RETREAT. The preached retreat involves major periods of time in which the leader presents the word of God in some type of "preached" manner. The rest of the time allows the retreatant to be alone for quiet reflection or to be with others for formal or informal activities.

The preached retreat format allows the leader to share the word with the maximum number of retreatants but allows minimum opportunity for the retreatant to receive personal direction from the retreat leader.

THE PRIVATE RETREAT. A private retreat is a time set apart for an individual to be alone for purposes of prayer and reflection. There are no others with whom to dialogue and no available guide to assist one's process. The retreatant must absolutely trust the Holy Spirit to serve as guide. A day regularly set apart for such purposes can be a powerful means of maintaining an awareness of the presence of God in one's life. There are many examples of private retreats in scripture; for example, Jesus spent forty days in private retreat following his baptism.

DECIDING THE CONTENT OF A RETREAT

Before we proceed to a lengthier discussion of each retreat form, we want to say something about deciding what to do in a retreat. First of all, a retreat leader needs to have a definite plan in mind that will give each retreatant a sense of going somewhere. You must have definite goals in mind regarding the "agenda" you want the retreatants to deal with through the process. "If you don't know where you are trying to get to, then any road will get you there," the rabbit told Alice in Wonderland.

Secondly, each of the various retreat forms is better suited both for persons at various stages in their own prayer development and for each of the pathways to spiritual maturity. It is our experience that persons who have not previously participated in dialogical retreats or who have not yet developed private disciplines of prayer and silence will find the extended times of solitude in a personally guided retreat to be frightening and intolerable.

Therefore, it is best for new retreatants to begin by attending one or two dialogical retreats. Usually these persons will begin to develop daily prayer disciplines naturally and will come to desire longer periods of silence and solitude. When this begins to happen, they will begin asking for retreat experiences that will allow more unstructured time and much longer periods to be alone. They are now ready for personally guided retreats, or day-long private retreats, and will no longer find dialogical retreats to be as helpful.

Also, it is our experience that persons need to talk with others about their life situations which are drawing them to the pathways of conversion or Christian service, while those who are being drawn to pathways of redemptive suffering or more mystical union with Christ will desire more time alone to get in touch with deeper levels of their interior selves.

Therefore, we have outlined dialogical retreat designs which will more naturally lead retreatants to consider those areas in their lives which are yet in need of repentance-conversion and to review how openly they are responding to the call to service.

The personally guided designs will more naturally lead persons to consider identifying with the redemptive sufferings of Christ and living in more intimate union with Christ.

By their very nature preached retreats are more closely aligned with dialogical forms, while private retreats seem to provide a dynamic bridge between dialogical and personally guided retreats.

With these considerations in mind, a suggested retreat schedule for a local church might therefore look like this:

1. Dialogical retreat, using one of the designs included in this book, or an Emmaus Walk.[1]

2. A six–to–nine–month period during which the retreatants develop a daily prayer discipline using the *Guide to Prayer for Ministers and Other Servants*, and meet in weekly or monthly groups to dialogue about their lives in Christ.

3. A dialogical retreat, Friday evening through Sunday.

4. A one–year period in which individuals continue the daily disciplines, with monthly meeting of the dialogue groups. Individuals begin monthly half–day or full–day private retreats.

5. A personally guided retreat.

6. Continue the daily disciplines, dialogue group, and monthly private retreat.

7. Ongoing schedule of steps 5 and 6.

3.

The Dialogical Retreat

"Then those who feared the Lord spoke to one another, and the Lord gave attention . . ." (Mal. 3:16, NASB). These words define the process and intent of dialogical retreats. Whenever God's people gather together to reflect upon and share their experiences, they discover that they are talking not only with each other but also with God.

The reflective conversation of persons in a common search for wholeness has a quality about it which draws Jesus into the conversation. This is what happened on the road to Emmaus. As two disciples were conversing with each other about the things that had taken place in their lives, Jesus joined them and entered into the conversation with them (Luke 24:15-16). This suggests some important aspects of both the leader's role and the retreatants' role in a dialogical retreat.

THE ROLE OF THE RETREAT LEADER

Providing topics and helps for the retreatants' reflection and dialogue. In order for persons to dialogue together, there must be a theme or focus for the conversation. The retreat leader provides a framework for the dialogue through the scripture selected for study, the brief input sessions, and the questions posed for reflection and group discussion.

Further, the leader must provide for a progression in the dialogue which will lead the retreatants to reflection upon and discussion of their experiences regarding the various basic concerns of the Christian life, as discussed in chapter 2.

Monitoring the group process. Some persons in dialogue groups need help in listening as another person shares emotional incidents and deep feelings. Such in-depth sharing may cause the listener to get in touch with repressed painful experiences in his or her own life, thus causing him or her to want to rescue the person from the emotional moment either by discounting the person's feelings, by changing the subject, or by giving advice. Of course, some persons are poor listeners simply because they spend too much time talking.

Fortunately, such situations in retreat groups are rare. The retreatants generally find appropriate patterns of listening and talking. However, when such situations do develop the retreat leader should not hesitate to instruct the group on more appropriate communication skills. We urge you, however, to do so only when you are convinced that communication patterns are consistently damaging the process for certain members of the group.

When you must intervene, let your words be brief and gentle. Keep in mind that you are conducting a spiritual life retreat, not a seminar in communication skills.

By constantly circulating among the groups, visiting each one for a few minutes to sense what is happening, you will know what is going on in each group and which ones may need more of your attention. Resist the efforts of the group to draw you into the conversation unless you are certain you have something helpful to add. Otherwise, simply say you are there as an "eavesdropper."

If the retreat has more groups than you can personally monitor, and if many of the retreatants are unfamiliar with elementary principles of group process, you may want to select and train a facilitator for each group.

Companioning the retreatant. There are usually some persons in each retreat who will especially benefit from one-to-one guidance from the leader. In some retreats there will be more persons wanting private time with you than you have time to provide. You should do only what you can without detracting from the retreat process.

The effectiveness of the time spent with individuals can be greatly enhanced if you have a clear picture of what it means to companion someone on their spiritual journey. Such a role involves three types of response—affirmation, challenge, and separation.

Affirmation: Affirm the retreatants as persons. Help them to know they are "special" to God. Affirm their efforts toward openness with God, themselves, and others. Affirm their freedom to follow the direction of the Spirit throughout the retreat.

Challenge: Challenge retreatants to confront honestly the dark side of their lives, the attitudes and behaviors which are frustrating their own search for wholeness. Challenge them to make decisions and to act upon them under the prompting of the Spirit.

Separation: Give retreatants the space needed to reflect upon their own experiences with God and others and on the new "agenda" which the Spirit is bringing to their attention. Give them the opportunity to decide their own response to all of that. Remember, each person must finally live his/her own life before God. There comes a point at which you have done all you **can** and **should** do. The rest is up to the individual.

We chose to use the word *separation* only after a long and arduous search for another word which might communicate more clearly. Having found none, we decided to use *separation*, assigning to it a very restricted and specific meaning.

If we look at biblical accounts of Jesus' relationship to those whom he companioned, we can find some of the same responses from Jesus. Following are two stories which will illustrate this point.

The story of the woman caught in adultery (John 8:1–11):

Affirmation: When the lawyers brought this woman to Jesus in the temple, you can be certain she was feeling unaffirmed and unacceptable. Soon, however, Jesus let her know that she was acceptable to him. Probably the most affirming words she had ever heard were, "Neither do I condemn you. . . ."

Challenge: He looked into her face for a spark of recognition that he loved her just as she was. As soon as he knew she felt his love he challenged the behavior that got her into trouble in the first place, "Sin no more," he told her (KJV). He wanted her to know that she need not continue her lifestyle; even though he accepted her as she was, she need not stay as she was.

Separation: Then Jesus told her in a single word that he trusted her to have the maturity and desire needed to change her life, "Go!" In that single word he told her, "You don't need me checking up on you every minute to see whether you are living up to my expectations. I believe you will on your own. Go now and make a new life for yourself."

The story of the two disciples on the road to Emmaus (Luke 24:13-31):

Affirmation: When Jesus came to walk with them, they weren't feeling too affirmed. In fact, as he joined them, "they stood still, looking sad," (v. 17, RSV). But he soon had them telling their story—and knowing that he deeply cared for them.

Challenge: After a while he began to challenge their ideas about what had happened. "How foolish you are, and how slow of heart to believe . . ." (v. 24, RSV).

Separation: At home, they invited Jesus in, and he sat down to eat with them. He affirmed them and their home with his gracious presence. He broke the bread and in this they recognized who he was. Immediately he disappeared from their sight (v. 31).

This wasn't a separation which said, "I don't accept you; I don't want to be with you, so I'm leaving." It was a separation that communicated, "Now that you know I'm alive, I trust you to know what to do." They got the message and acted on it (vv. 33-35).

Hosting the process in the name of the Lord. It is important for the leader and the retreatant to remember that the Holy Spirit is the true leader of the retreat. Perhaps "usher" or "host" would be a better term for the person responsible for the retreat.

Consider two types of "directing": the traffic officer on the corner and a restaurant host/hostess. When you ask directions from the officer neither you nor the officer expects the officer to go with you. It would be wonderful if the officer would, but traffic at that corner is the officer's responsibility. Your "lostness" is not a major concern. The officer may give you a map and point in the right direction, but won't leave the corner to accompany you.

The restaurant host or hostess, on the other hand, will meet you at the door and usher you through the maze of tables to the one he or she wants you to have. If, however, you choose to go another direction, to sit at a different table, you have the freedom to do so.

This latter way of directing is the model for a sensitive retreat leader. Have a plan in mind for the retreatants and accompany them through it. If, however, a retreatant chooses to go another direction, give him or her the freedom to do so and provide directions to make that "way" refreshing and full of growth potential.

You may do this without any sense of ill will or loss of self-confidence in the plan you have developed. If the Holy Spirit is indeed the true leader, it is to be expected that from time to time the Spirit will direct a retreatant to go in a particular direction. For example, a retreatant may feel the need for more solitude and may wish to drop out of the group for an hour or more. Affirm the retreatant's attempt to listen to the Spirit and invite him or her to return to the group when the Spirit leads in that direction.

We have had persons attend an entire retreat who have followed the process only when the total group was together for content input. Then in the final moments of the retreat they have testified to life-changing decisions made during their time alone with God.

The retreat leader is, however, more than a host or hostess. The leader is also an encourager, a spiritual guide, a monitor of the process, and a companion on the journey.

THE ROLE OF THE RETREATANT

The retreatant's role is to present him/herself frankly and honestly before God in the periods of private reflection and to enter into the dialogue sessions with openness in sharing and an "ear" toward God's word as it is heard in the heartfelt sharing of the group members. This is not to say that retreatants should feel compelled to disclose all that came to them during times of private reflection. Indeed, it is the retreatants' freedom and responsibility to share only that which they feel God would have them share.

The retreat leader should make this clear early in the retreat. When persons realize they are under no compulsion to disclose publicly all they are experiencing and praying about, they experience a greater freedom to be absolutely honest with themselves and God in the private times. This honesty with self and God in private strengthens retreatants to enter into deep, spirit-led dialogue with the group.

When persons are convinced they have unconditional permission to be absolutely silent in the group, they then experience a freedom to share at intensely personal levels. Since the retreatants are responsible for monitoring their own depth of self–disclosure, the leader should be reluctant to protect persons from sharing too much.

A concern expressed by many new retreat leaders is that persons will share too much and be sorry later. We have never seen this happen in a spiritual life retreat where persons know they are free to share as much, or as little, as they wish. We do find that most persons prefer not to be in groups with their spouses and that the depth of personal disclosure is often greater in groups comprised of persons that do not all belong to the same congregation. But in any group the depth of sharing is usually deep, open, and heartfelt.

GUIDELINES FOR PLANNING AND CONDUCTING
A DIALOGICAL RETREAT

We urge retreat planners and leaders to follow a few important guidelines.

1. Don't pack the retreat "work" schedule too tightly. Leave room for relaxation, recreation, or simply "cleaning out" thoughts and emotions.

Plan time for retreatants to mentally digest materials being covered. This allows opportunity for the subconscious to send messages to the conscious. The retreatant needs this kind of time to deal with the material. This kind of time also allows other information to drop into the subconscious for future use.

The desert fathers called retreat times "wasting time with God." For work–oriented people unscheduled time will feel like a waste of time, but it is for a good purpose and God will use it for the retreatants' spiritual growth.

Packing the schedule too tightly is a bugaboo we still have to work with in our own retreats. There is always another Bible story we want to tell, another exercise or film we want to use. Often we must remind ourselves that Jesus took the disciples away on retreat to "rest a while," not to burden them with another taxing schedule (Mark 6:31, RSV).

2. The most effective dialogical retreat will keep the group together for at least two overnights. Although we cannot explain all the dynamics, our experience confirms that having a group together for a second overnight results in quantum differences in results on all fronts. Undoubtedly, one reason for this ties back to the first guideline. The additional time in the retreat allows the leader to relax the schedule while still covering the retreat agenda. A three-day retreat does not need to include much additional material from that of a two-day retreat. Rather, the material can be spread out in a more relaxed fashion.

Often, however, circumstances are such that you cannot have a three-day retreat. Then work with as much time as you have. Even a very short retreat can meet your expectations—if your expectations are not too high. God indeed works miracles, but growth-type miracles require time.

3. The retreat experience will always be enhanced by taking the group away from home and church settings to a "place apart" where they can live, play, and work together.

The entire experience loses much when the retreat is held in the church building, and the retreatants separate to their various homes for the night. The movement back into their homes, families, and telephones results in a disjointed retreat experience.

4. The setting for the retreat should be selected to facilitate the process and goals of the retreat. The dialogical retreat, for example, requires places for quietness and solitude as well as places for the discussion group to meet for quiet conversation. In addition, there should be a meditation chapel.

Keep in mind that adults require different facilities for comfort and rest than do teenagers. Regular church camp facilities with dormitory rooms, broken–down bunk beds, and rusty showers are often so unfamiliar and distasteful for North American adults that they are deprived of adequate rest and the space they need for quiet reflection and time alone.

Only twice have we had to deal with interpersonal conflict among retreatants. Both instances involved situations in which women were forced to sleep together in dormitory settings and one woman snored loudly! In one instance, three women moved out into their cars in the middle of a frosty night to escape the snoring. Before we could begin the session the following morning a bit of conflict resolution was necessary!

Also, watch your menu. Heavy, starchy food makes persons feel drowsy and "heavy." This is hardly the way you want persons to feel in an important afternoon retreat session.

5. Guard against the temptation to give too much scripture content in your talks, or in the agenda for private reflection and group discussion. Don't preach except in a preached retreat, and offer guidance sparingly except in a personally guided retreat.

Perhaps the most common problem facing retreat leaders is an ego need to be spectacular, to be wiser than the retreatants. The model of Christ gives us good insight—he gave few answers to direct questions and left most stories incomplete in order to encourage persons to search for answers and to find solutions on their own.

6. Use Bible stories when introducing a new theme for reflection and dialogue—just learn the story and tell it. Don't talk about it, or "preach" about it. If you do, the danger is that you will give too much information, thus boxing the retreatants in so they will think and feel about the story as you do. This denies the Spirit the opportunity to lead each one into an intensely personal confrontation with the Word as it is speaking to his/her own life situation.

Over the years, we have used many forms of story–telling in retreats—fantasy, drama, casting the story in contemporary settings. Slowly we have come to understand that simply telling the story from scripture is perhaps the preferred method in retreat settings. Scripture stories carry their own inspiration and power. They can stand on their own. They need no new twist or embellishment.

It is not essential that you memorize the story word-for-word. What is required is that you know the story well enough to tell it with intonation and force.

Actually you need not, and in some cases should not, tell the story. Simply give the reference, tell the retreatants what you want them to meditate upon, and let them be their own storytellers. St. Ignatius thought this was the best method of all, since it gives the Spirit more freedom to suggest to the retreatant what he/she should see in the scripture. On some occasions you may simply choose to read the story.

There are, of course, times when you will use non-story scriptures (e.g., Phil. 4:4–17; sections from Matt. 5–7; Rom. 6;7-12).

7. Don't answer many questions! Often your answer to a question releases the person from the necessary tension to resolve an issue God wants them to confront. Answers in

dialogical retreats come from the Spirit in the retreatant's solitude and in the group discussions. The stories you tell, the assignments you give, and the group discussions raise the questions; the retreatant finds the answer in the times of aloneness with God or in the word shared in the group.

8. Be open, transparent, and relaxed. If you want the people to share their life experiences and to be open to the Spirit, you must set the climate by your own behavior. The retreatants will follow your lead.

9. Use music that connects with the memories of the retreatants and/or which touches their deepest religious emotions.[1] Don't use flimsy choruses simply because they have a singable melody. Whether hymns, gospel songs, or choruses, choose them carefully to connect with the basic concern of the Christian life you are emphasizing at the moment. For example, "O Love That Wilt Not Let Me Go" connects with the concern of the love of God.

Don't be afraid to use the same song several times in a retreat.

PLANNING A DIALOGICAL RETREAT

We put our designs together in sessions, each of which "hangs" together with its preceding and following session in such a way that one session may be taken out and another inserted without changing other sessions. Then as we work with a group and come to know what the retreatants are dealing with, we will often change the scripture, meditation process, or group assignment in order to target the retreat content to where the group is.

Following are three dialogical retreat designs which will work in a variety of settings and groups. We will tell you where we have tended to use each design; however, you should feel free to adapt them to whatever retreat setting and group in which you find yourself.

DIALOGICAL RETREAT DESIGN 1

Conditions Suggesting This Design:

1. **Group Size:**   4 to 45 persons
2. **Type of audience:**   General
3. **Length of retreat:**   Evening, plus one and one-half days, or two full days

---

SCHEDULE

Session 1: Setting the Stage
FIRST DAY

TIME	ACTIVITY	NOTES
7:00 P.M.	**Total Group** *Opening Worship* Housekeeping Announcements: Brief! Psalm 63 Hymn Singing **Prayer:** The Lord's Prayer (In unison) Scripture Reading: Mark 6:30-32 Jesus realized his friends had been working hard at their ministry and decided to take them on retreat. Two themes here describe the place and purpose of retreats: "A lonely place." We are to leave our busy, familiar surroundings for an unhurried, relaxed atmosphere. "Rest a while." We are to relax and rest here. Retreats are to renew, not fatigue, us. Do not work at the	You may allow the group to choose a few favorites and conclude with "Come, Thou Almighty King" A time of clarifying our own needs and focusing our own desires for this retreat

38

TIME	ACTIVITY	NOTES

agenda, but approach it as children approach play.

Time of clarifying our own needs and focusing our own desire for this retreat

7:30 P.M.
(10 minutes)

Story-telling:

Blind Bartimaeus (Mark 10:46-52). Jews could not stand to look at a leper or into a blind person's eyes, so the blind wore a cloak over their eyes. Blind Bartimaeus threw the cloak away. He came just as he was for Jesus to see. We must come "open–faced" to the Christ who calls us in love, and make our requests in faith.

(15 minutes)

Alone Time

Imagine Jesus is here and asks you: "What do you want me to do for you?"

Prayerfully reflect upon and write your response to this question.

Allow persons to move to a place anywhere in the building for their reflection time.

(30 minutes)

Dyad

Share your response with another person. What heart's desires did you find yourself reflecting on during your alone time?

8:25 P.M.

Total Group

(10 minutes)

"What was it like to share and to listen to your personal desires?"

(3 minutes)

Silent Prayer for Jesus to Grant Our Desires.

Each person pray for their dyad partner.

(2 minutes)

Morning Bible Study Assignment

See next page for assignment.

8:40 P.M.

END OF FIRST DAY

SCHEDULE

Session 2: You Are Loved Just As You Are
SECOND DAY

TIME	ACTIVITY	NOTES
7:45 A.M.	**Dyads or Roommate Groups** **Alone Bible Study** The Prodigal Father (Luke 15:11-32) Prayerfully *study the scripture* and jot down your responses to the following questions: 1. What does this scripture tell me about God? 2. What does this scripture tell me about the way humans tend to be? 3. In what sense is this story my story? Where do I find myself in this scripture?	In some instances it will seem best not to have an assignment before breakfast.
8:00 A.M. *(15 minutes)*	**Group Discussion** Discuss your response to the questions.	
8:15 A.M.	Breakfast	
9:00 A.M. *(10 minutes)*	**Total Group** Opening Worship Psalm 62 Hymn: "O Love That Wilt Not Let Me Go" Prayer: The Lord's Prayer	

(10 minutes)

Before Proceeding: Have the group divide itself into groups of four persons each. Allow persons to self-select their groups and decide where they will meet for their group discussions. After groups are formed, ask persons to be seated and continued.	*Emphasize:* In all group sharing times, share only what you want to. It's okay to be silent in the group. You need not tell the group all you thought about or wrote in the alone time—but share all that you care to. Give strong permission for spouses to go to separate groups, but do not insist. Use the same groups of four throughout the retreat.

TIME	ACTIVITY	NOTES
9:20 A.M.	**Story-telling:** The Story of the Prodigal Father (Luke 15:11-31)	Assignment continued in afternoon session.

TIME	ACTIVITY	NOTES

9:35 A.M.

Assignment

"Remembering" our own journey

Construct the trail of your past religious experience by identifying and jotting down your responses to the following questions:

1. At what point did you begin to consider God as a serious factor in your life situations?
2. What was perhaps the most serious and consequential commitment you ever made to God?
3. At what points in your life has God seemed most near?
4. At what points in your life has God seemed farthest away?

NOTE: For your response to each question jot down:

What were the circumstances?

Who were important persons in the circumstances?

When was it and *where* were you?

Why is it important to you now?

How is it important to you now?

Assignment continued in afternoon session.

9:40 A.M. **Alone Time**

Allow persons to find a quiet place anywhere they may wish.

(20 minutes) Reflect on the questions and jot down your responses.

10:00 A.M. Move to small groups.
Pick up coffee and snacks along the way.

10:20 A.M. **Groups of four**

(60 minutes) Discuss your responses to the questions.

11:20 A.M. Move to total group—hurry!

11:30 A.M. **Total Group**

General Discussion
1. What was it like to "re-member" your past experiences?

<u>TIME</u>	<u>ACTIVITY</u>	<u>NOTES</u>

2. What was it like to hear the others' stories?

3. What insights did you gain?

11:50 A.M.   BREAK

THE TIME FROM 11:50 A.M.
TO 3:00 P.M. IS FREE TIME!!

Session 3: Walking with the Lord: From Darkness into the Light,
From Unfreedom to Freedom, From Sin to Salvation

3:00 P.M.   **Total Group**
Hymn singing
Psalm 139:1-12, 23-24
Hymn: "Search Me, O God"

3:20 P.M.   **Story-telling:**
(15 minutes)   Zacchaeus: Steps from Sin to
Salvation (Luke 19:1-10)

3:35 P.M.   **Assignment**

(5 minutes)   Taking a look at the present
condition of our Christian life
This morning we reflected on our
past life. Now we want to look at
the "here and now" of our
Christian experience to see what
connections there may be
between the past and the present
("re-membering" our experiences).
We will do this by reflecting on
three questions:

1. What word(s) would I use to
describe the present condition
of my Christian life?

2. What are the blockages/
hindrances to my spiritual
growth?

3. What steps might I take, even
now, to reduce the obstacles to
my own Christian growth?

3:40 P.M.   **Alone Time**

(20 minutes)   Reflect on the questions and jot
down your responses.

42

TIME	ACTIVITY	NOTES
4:00 P.M.	Move to small groups. Pick up drink along the way.	
4:20 P.M.	**Groups of four**	
(70 minutes)	Share your responses to the questions.	
5:30 P.M.	BREAK	

SCHEDULE

Session 4: You Are Chosen to Help Make the Kingdom Vision Come True

7:00 P.M.	**Prayerful Reflection** A time to reflect on what has been happening in the retreat.	

TIME	ACTIVITY	NOTES
(20 minutes)	**Alone Bible Study** (John 15:1-8, 16) Prayerfully study the scripture and jot down your responses to the following questions: 1. What does this scripture tell me about God? 2. What does it tell me about the human tendency of things? 3. Where do I find myself in this story? 4. What does God seem to be saying to me about my life, even now? Then—	
(5 minutes)	Write a letter (a prayer) to God in two brief paragraphs regarding: 1. What I have experienced and learned about myself in the re- treat. 2. What I intend to do about those learnings. Then—	

TIME	ACTIVITY	NOTES

(5 minutes) — Write a letter (a meditation) from God to you about how God seems to be responding to your letter.

NOTES:

Example:
To Norm,

_____

_____

_____

Signed: God

(This is one method of the "prayer of imagination," and is in keeping with the tradition of God's speaking to persons in dreams, visions, and impulses.)

7:30 P.M. — Move to total group—hurry!

7:40 P.M.

Total Group

(30 minutes)

Lecture:
"The Spiritual Disciplines: Putting the pieces of the puzzle together." The disciplines are means of making ourselves available to be "united with Christ" and to maintain a consistent sense of connectedness.

These disciplines are:
Doorways to freedom and adventure in the Christian life:

Inward: prayer, meditation, study, fasting, solitude/silence

Outward: service, submission, simplicity

Corporate: worship, guidance, confession, celebration

God alone gives us growth and life. The disciplines are doorways, not an end in themselves.

NOTES:

Resource: Richard Foster, *The Celebration of Discipline* (San Francisco: Harper & Row, 1978).

All of these involve *risk*. We must come to them freely and under no obligation. We must not feel guilt-ridden when we fail in our pledges to keep them.

8:10 P.M.

Assignment

(5 minutes)

Taking stock of the Christian disciplines in your own life:
1. Which disciplines have I already developed in my life? To what degree?

44

TIME	ACTIVITY	NOTES

2. Which disciplines have I not developed? What is blocking me from doing so even now?

3. In order to do this, what changes would I need to make in my life?

4. What help will I need from others? From whom?

8:15 P.M. **Alone Time**

(15 minutes) Reflect on the questions and jot down your responses.

8:30 P.M. **Groups of four**

(30 minutes) Discuss your responses to the questions.

9:00 P.M. END OF SECOND DAY

SCHEDULE

THIRD DAY

8:15 A.M. Breakfast

9:00 A.M. **Total Group**
Opening Worship
Psalm 91
Hymn: "How Great Thou Art"
Prayer: The Lord's Prayer

9:15 A.M. **Discussion of Yesterday's Experience:**

(15 minutes)
1. What was the most important insight, experience for you?

2. What was your experience in writing a letter to God? In writing God's reply to you?

9:30 A.M. **Reflections on Mark 6:33-44**

(15 minutes) In this story Jesus did two things:

1. He gave the disciples a new glimpse into the kingdom of

TIME	ACTIVITY	NOTES

God—all the hungry can be filled (Matt. 5:6).

2. He showed them their important place in making the kingdom vision come true, "You feed them."

- Disciples wanted to send the people away, to make them, or someone else, responsible for their need . . .

- Because they felt inadequate; they had nothing to offer.

- Jesus said, "No, you feed them."

- They gave the five loaves and two fish to *Jesus*, not to the crowd.

- He blessed it, and broke it, and gave it back to them for the crowd.

- That is the secret of effective service, to be always offering what little we have to Christ, that he may bless us and break us for others and for the needs of the world around us.

- The secret of the kingdom is that we may not have much, but with Christ it's always enough to meet the great needs. He has equipped each of us for an important service.

This is *your* story of how to be effective in *your* own life of service.

9:45 A.M.
(5 minutes) — **Alone Time**
A Time of Silent Reflection

(5 minutes) — Write whatever comes to your mind.

(5 minutes) — Silent Prayer. Lift what you have written as a prayer to God.

10:00 A.M. — Move to small groups; pick up refreshments along the way.

10:15 A.M.
(45 minutes) — **Groups of Four**
A time of wrap-up discussion

1. What I gained from this retreat.

2. How I plan to "use" this experience back home.

TIME	ACTIVITY	NOTES

AND FINALLY

3. How may we minister to each other here in this group before we return to the total group?

11:00 A.M. Move to total group—hurry!

11:10 A.M. **Total Group**

Closing Worship
Hymn: "O Master, Let Me Walk with Thee"
Scripture: Isaiah 6:1–9*a*
  Jeremiah 1:4–9

Homily:

1. God has spoken to us here.

2. Do not say, "I cannot do it." Do not resist the message of God to you.

3. God will go with you, and nothing is impossible with God (Luke 1:37).

Eucharist or Love Feast

For Love Feast, see next page.

Passing of the Peace

END OF RETREAT

A Form for Use in Observance of the Love Feast

Traditionally, worshipers were seated in a circle or around a table. A common loaf was passed from hand to hand. A loving cup with two handles was provided for water, but later individual glasses were used, and a pitcher was passed from hand to hand.

A Hymn of Praise

The Scripture (John 6:26–35 or Mal. 3:16–17)

Voluntary Prayers and the Lord's Prayer

An Address

A Hymn of Christian Fellowship

The Passing of the Bread
  Here this blessing shall be said: "Blessed art thou, O Lord, God of the universe, who dost bring forth bread from the earth. Amen."

Offering for the Poor

The Passing of The Cup
  Here this promise shall be said: "Jesus Christ said, 'Whosoever drinketh of the water that I shall give him shall never thirst.' Amen."

A Thanksgiving in Unison (to be said by all):
  Blessed art thou, O God, the author of all sustenance, who hast nourished us from our youth up. Fill, we beseech thee, our hearts with joyfulness, that in thy bountiful providence we may serve thee with every good work; through Jesus Christ our Lord, to whom with thee and the Holy Ghost be all glory and power, honor and worship, both now and forevermore. Amen.

Testimonies

A Hymn of Thanksgiving

A Blessing

DIALOGICAL RETREAT DESIGN 2

Conditions Suggesting This Design:

1. **Group Size:**   100 to 500 persons
2. **Type of Audience:**   General
3. **Length of Retreat:**   One evening and one day

SCHEDULE

Session 1: Setting the Stage
FIRST DAY

TIME	ACTIVITY	NOTES
2:00–5:30 P.M.	**Registration**	In this column give instructions regarding meeting rooms, names of speakers, and other details.
4:30 P.M.	***Training Session** for those serving as enablers	
6:00 P.M.	**Dinner** Welcome and instructions for table discussions.	

Table Discussions
  • Each person introduces him/herself. Tell why you came to retreat, and what you hope to gain from it. Be as specific as possible.

7:30 P.M.   **Total Group**

Opening Worship

Welcome and Announcements
Psalm 139
Hymn Singing

*See page 53 for information regarding keyed items.

TIME	ACTIVITY	NOTES

8:00 P.M.   ****"_____"**
                (Keynote Address)

9:00 P.M.   Dismiss to Refreshments

END OF FIRST EVENING

Session 2: You Are Loved by God Just as You Are

SECOND DAY

8:30 A.M.   **Total Group**

           Opening Worship
           Psalm 91
           The Lord's Prayer
           Hymn Singing

8:45 A.M.   **Story-telling:**
           The Prodigal Father (Luke 15:11-32)

           Silent Reflection

           Hymn: "O Love That Wilt Not Let Me Go"

9:10 A.M.   *"The Story of a Prodigal Daughter (or Son)"

           Silent Reflection

           **Hymn: "Amazing Grace"

9:50 A.M.   Move to Small Groups

10:10 A.M.   **Small Groups**

           (Your group number is on your name tag. See handout sheet for meeting place.)

(10 minutes)   Silent Reflection:

           1. How is it with your soul today?
           2. Do you desire to serve God with your whole heart?
           3. Do you have full assurance that God loves you and that your sins are forgiven?

These are traditional questions written by John Wesley for the early Methodist "bands" and have been used for over two hundred years.

(45 minutes)   Discussion of the Questions

(10 minutes)   Silent Reflection

(15 minutes)   Wrap–Up Discussion:

           What insights came to you during the silence?

           How might this group minister to you just now?

TIME	ACTIVITY	NOTES
11:30 A.M.	**Break**	
12:00 Noon	**Lunch**	

Session 3: Walking with Jesus
From Darkness into the Light, From Unfreedom to Freedom

1:30 P.M.	**Total Group**	
(15 minutes)	Hymn Singing	
(10 minutes)	"The Three Journeys toward a Balanced Christian Life"	Resource: Shawchuck, *What It Means to Be a Church Leader* (Spiritual Growth Resources.)

    • The journey into your inner self, where you live alone, in secret. The intrapersonal dimension of your Christian life.

    • The journey with family, friends, congregation, where you have relationships with persons closest to you. The interpersonal dimension of your Christian life.

    • The journey into the world, where you offer your life in service to God and others. The public dimension of your Christian life.

(10 minutes)	**Story-telling:** Zacchaeus Moves from Darkness into the Light (Luke 19:1–10)	
(5 minutes)	Silent Reflection	
2:10 P.M.	Move to Small Groups	
2:30 P.M.	**Small Groups**	Your group number is on your name tag. See handout sheet for meeting place.
(5 minutes)	Introduction to the Session	
(5 minutes)	Silent Reflection	

    The Journey into Yourself (Ps. 139:23–24, RSV) Search me, O God, and know my heart! Try me and know my thoughts! And see if there be any wicked way in me, and lead me in the way everlasting.

Questions for reflection

    1. When you search deep into my

TIME	ACTIVITY	NOTES

secret life, O Lord, what do you see?

2. What is the true condition of my inner, secret life?

(20 minutes)   Open Discussion of the quality of the inner life you are experiencing with God.

3:00 P.M.   BREAK

3:05 P.M.
(5 minutes)   **Return to Small Groups**
Introduction to the Session

(10 minutes)   Silent Reflection: Putting it all together to establish a vibrant, balanced Christian life (Rom. 12:1–2; Eph. 5:1, RSV)

> I urge you therefore, brethren, by the mercies of God, to present your bodies as a living sacrifice, holy and acceptable to God, which is your spiritual worship. Do not be conformed to this world, but be transformed by the renewing of your mind, that you may prove what is the will of God, what is good and acceptable and perfect. Therefore be imitators of God, as beloved children.

Question for Reflection:
What in particular, O God who created the universe, do you want me to do about my Christian life and witness, even now?

(40 minutes)   Open Discussion of what God seems to be saying to you, and the direction God is "nudging" just now.

4:00 P.M.   BREAK

5:00 P.M.   **Dinner**

6:15 P.M.   **Total Group**

Closing Service
*Eucharist
Hymn
Sermon: "Call to Service and
  Commitment"
Sending Forth

END OF RETREAT

INFORMATION KEY

Session 1

*1. Through registration process assign each retreatant to a group, seven in each group.

2. Recruit an enabler for each group.

3. Training Session—Enablers' task
   • Help all retreatants find their room locations.
   • Keep the clock—start and end group on time.
   • Give instructions for the period.
   • Note: The best enabler is one who can keep the group running smoothly without anyone's being aware a special "enabler" is in the room.
   • But take control when you must.
   • Do not "rescue" persons and don't allow others to do so. Do not be afraid of emotions. Do not let one person dominate time or correct others.

**The Keynote Address is crucial to the entire retreat since it "sets the stage" for all that follows. It need not be an "address," but may be a drama, liturgy, or some other form. Whatever is done must be carefully prepared to set the stage for all that follows. Use no one who has not been acquainted with the goals and audience of this event. An example of a keynote address follows.

Session 2

* Invite a layperson to give witness of his or her journey away from and back to the Creator. This person must be able to speak before a large crowd, but not "polished."

** Solo (perhaps "Amazing Grace") or hymn.

Session 3

* Plan Eucharist to be "serious" but "different"—one that will allow persons to gather up all the emotions and impulses felt during the retreat in order to respond fully to the call to service and commitment.

Additional considerations for planning a large retreat:

1. Select site far in advance. We prefer a convention center with an adjacent h/motel, or a motel with a large meeting room.

2. Use retreatants' motel rooms for "small groups." The need for persons to sit on chairs, beds, or floor creates an ideal informal atmosphere.

3. Have some small rooms adjacent to the meeting hall for persons with handicapping conditions and elderly retreatants.

4. Require registration in advance in order to make small group and room assignments.

5. It will be necessary to print a retreat manual for each retreatant. Include such information as:

Information sheet which gives:
   • information regarding eating
   • information regarding small group assignments
   • directions to various locations
   • directions when problems or emergencies arise
   • provision for lost and found area

Retreat design (complete)

Song sheet(s)

Texts of all scripture

Names and addresses of retreat leadership, staff, and sponsoring group

Names and addresses of retreatants

Six blank "Notes" pages

The Arena of Spiritual Formation
A Keynote Address

What are we about in this meeting?
   What do we hope to achieve?

What did we bring with us to this meeting?
   What yearnings? Thirsts? Hungers?
      What sense of inadequacy? Weakness?

What sense of hope?
   What new song is beginning its melody
      even as we gather here together?
         What joyous expectations?

We are now here—together—
   Men and women in common search—
      responding to a common invitation.

And whatever the surface reasons, whatever
   The visible cause—

We must now believe we are here because
   God invited us,
      Because the Sovereign Host has
         prepared a banquet,

And sent the servants to tell us
   our names are on the honored
      guest list!

We must believe we are here
   Because this is where we belong.

And the God who invited us is well
   able to care for us now that we have come.

Now that we have come
   God is well able
      to feed our hungers,
         to fill our time,
   to care for us,
      and to grant us our heart's desire!

I suppose we are all here because we hope
   in our hearts to be renewed—
      and that we may find something here
         to help renew our church.

But where can we look for clues to
   point us in the direction of renewal
      for ourselves and the church?

We know now that the clues do not
   point us toward more programs, or
      plans, or administrative restructure.

The clues do not point toward more debate,
   or greater frenzy,
      or harder work, or longer hours.

The clues to renewal are pointing today
   where they have always pointed . . .

They are directing us inward—
   into the quiet caverns of our own hearts,
      to unhurried conversations with
         the Christ hidden within,
            to covenant communities of men
               and women who are willing to
                  support one another,
                     and provide accountability for one another,
                        as they confront the obstacles
which stand in their way to a renewed life and church!

We are at the present time in the
   midst of some kind of spiritual explosion,
      the growing force of which seems to be
         more of an implosion—
            a drawing of persons back into
their interior lives.

There is a call of the Spirit going out
   that is being heard by persons in
      increasing numbers as a call
         to greater interiority.

For several decades the American and
   European church has searched for
      God in things external—

In greater programs,
   more ambitious projects,
      in larger crusades,
         in demonstrations, and sacrifices,
and in our own ministerial appointments.
But somehow these have served only to
   leave us tired,
      and disillusioned, and stressful
         and discouraged, and broken.

And now it is beginning to dawn on us
   that spirituality and ministry are
      not the same.

That ministry provides us the field in
   which to work for the kingdom
      of God—

But

Spirituality provides us the force,
    the stamina, and vision
necessary to keep us from being consumed
    by the trivia of the daily grind, or
from being overwhelmed by the forces of darkness
    which everywhere confront and
        frustrate our most valiant efforts.

Now it is beginning to dawn upon us
    that the life and energy for which
        we seek,
            and for which we stand in
    such desperate need,

can only be found within,
    and "comes to us only in drastic
        changes in our own relations with
        one another, and through yielding
        ever fresh areas of our own life
        to God, areas that until this
        time have been withheld." (*Douglas V. Steere*)

Now please understand me!

I am not saying that we should abandon our
    activist ministries for
        a religious experience that leads
            us along a one–way street
                inward!

Far from it!

Actually, I believe if you can only
    travel one way in your religious
        experience,
    you should then travel outward
        into activist encounter with
            dishonesty, hatred, and injustice
                in whatever system or
                    form you find it.
    And you should engage the struggle
        until your reserves are depleted,
            and you collapse in
    utter exhaustion,
        and your light goes out.

For you see,
    I am thoroughly convinced that the
        Sovereign Lord,
            Judge of all persons,
    will smile more benevolently upon

56

the activist burn-out
    than upon
the quietist shut-in.

What I am trying to say is that
    ministry and spirituality are not the same!
    Ministry and spirituality are different
        from each other—
            But
    they are interrelated and
        interdependent upon each other.

We know this—
    or at least we are beginning to
        suspect this.

And so in our own beloved United Methodist Church
    there is beginning an explosion of sorts
        under the rubric of *spiritual formation*.

In many areas persons are asking questions
    about the quality of our life together,
        are naming the fears which
            plague our ministries,
are confessing our loneliness.

In many areas, persons are beginning to
    search for a more vital piety
        to sustain our activist ministry.

We are coming together out of our own
    sense of need.
We are beginning to pool our handicaps
    to see whether we can fix up
        our two hundred–year–old house and
            live in it!
We should not be too surprised at
    this phenomenon in United Methodism!
This invitation of the Spirit is coming to us at the
    moment of our most critical need—

And our need is our qualification for renewal!

Archbishop William Temple is reported to have said,
    "It is an unalterable fact of history
        that when the church is most dead,
        from out of its own body God will
        raise up new life."

And so the invitation to a banquet
    is going out from the playful and
        eccentric One who
            delights in inviting the cripples

to the banquet hall,
  and who
    delights in getting inside us
to rummage around in the closeted
  affairs of our secret selves
    to discover a long–buried
      germ of life—
and then promptly, patiently begins
  to nurture it.

From deep within our own experience
  God is speaking, calling, cajoling . . .

This is a *kairos* moment for us
  who are called United Methodist—
    a moment pregnant with
      opportunity–and danger.

• There is the danger that our search for a more vital piety should culminate in a
  spiritual narcissism—that having begun the journey inward we should avoid the
  journey outward.

  We can avoid this only by grounding our search in the dialectic of being called back to
  the "core" of our being and of being sent out into the rough and tumble challenges
  and risks of active ministry in an increasingly secular, hostile world.

• There is the danger that
  we will attempt to make
the journey alone.
    If renewal is to come to
  our two hundred–year–old house,
  it will require drastic changes in
    our relationships with one another.

It will require a "coming together,"
  a laying down of our petty dis-trusts,
    power struggles, and
      our fierce independence
which shut us off from one another.

Christian spirituality is a
  communal spirituality.
We cannot renew ourselves, or
  our stations of ministry, alone.

We need covenant communities,
  "Christian Conference," for
    Support and
    Accountability.

• There is the danger that we will
  dilute the importance of
spiritual formation,

TOOLS FOR DESIGNING AND CONDUCTING SPIRITUAL LIFE RETREATS

or of our own experience
in an attempt to be accepted,
        or to appear respectable in all circles
            of Christian idealogy.

For, you see, there is a concomitant danger that

• the organized church will not
        accept or tolerate
            spiritual formation,
will see it as unimportant, or
        as a threat to special interests
            and prevailing practices.

John Wesley wanted to revivify the
Anglican Church in his time.
    He succeeded only in being, himself,
expelled from its pulpits
                    and
    in fostering a missionary movement
which broke away from the church
a few days after his death!

• But for most of us
        the greatest danger is that
            we will want the results
                of spiritual formation
                    without its disciplines

Augustine was correct when he said:
"We come to God by love, and not navigation."

And John Wesley was correct when he
insisted that God's grace is a
prevenient grace.

Jesus is always moving toward us—
long before we even knew, or cared!

But John Wesley also left us with
an understanding of
        the means of grace—
the means by which grace comes, and
the means by which we open ourselves
    to the grace that is already available—

So we Methodists have inherited a
tradition with paradox.

The grace is already given quite
without our counsel or consent
                            but

    it is a grace which can be
resisted

therefore
There are means by which we can
present ourselves open to it
and
The same means by which grace
presents itself available to us.
The means are, according to Wesley:

Instituted	Prudential
Prayer	Acts of mercy
Searching the scripture	Avoiding all harm
Fasting	to anyone
The Lord's Supper	Attending all the
Christian Conference	ordinances of God

And so we give ourselves to them—
And soon find ourselves crying,
"How can anything which
promises such graceful delights
prove to be itself such drudgery?"

Every profession, every worthwhile
endeavor has its own unique set
of concomitant disciplines,
and
the common denominator which
separates
growing persons from
stagnant persons
is this:
Stagnant persons focus upon easy and
pleasing methods;
growing persons focus upon desired
results.

We are here in this place
to focus upon desired results
and to reflect for a while
upon the meaning and importance
of the means of grace for our own lives.
I think the words of Wesley to
one of the preachers are appropriate
for us:

"O BEGIN! Fix some part of every day for private
exercises. . . . Whether you like it or no, read and
pray daily. It is for your life; there is no
other way; else you will be a trifler all your
days."

So—for the next three days—let's just
   BE here. God's grace has
preceded us to this place
    the Banquet was prepared *before*
      our coming
            and
    for our coming.
And the God who brought you here
is well able to feed and
         care for you,
           and
  fill all your hours while
you are here.

DIALOGICAL RETREAT DESIGN 3

Conditions Suggesting This Design:

1. **Group Size:** 10 to 100 persons
2. **Type of Audience:** Group sharing common vocation within a formal structure
3. **Length of Retreat:** Two full days (48 hours)
4. **Special Features:** Time for group discernment and a plan for covenant living.

Session 1: Setting the Stage
FIRST DAY

TIME	ACTIVITY	NOTES
12:00-1:00 P.M.	**Registration**	Use this column to identify leader, room assignment, and other details.
2:00 P.M.	**Opening Worship** Welcome Hymn: "Come, Thou Almighty King" Psalm 42 "Why this event was called— hopes and goals" Overview of Design Prayer	
2:30 P.M.	**Setting the Stage for the Retreat Experience** • God brought us here; God will care for us, feed us here. • Retreats are an old tradition	

62

TIME	ACTIVITY	NOTES

within Christian experience (Mark 6:30-32).
• Two frames of mind can define approaches to a retreat:
  • Sandbox
  • Adventure Trail

There is a little bit of sandbox and adventure trail in each of us. Stay on the adventure trail all you can; get back into the sandbox when you must. Rest awhile, then join us on the trail again.

2:45 P.M.   **Group Reflection** (Luke 5:1-11)

1. They had toiled hard in the old familiar places and had caught nothing.
2. They were following the rules, "You catch fish in shallow waters!"
3. Jesus led them into deep, "unlikely" water.
4. They did catch fish, but Peter caught a new insight into himself and into who Jesus was (v. 8), and this insight caused him to want to accept, "O Lord," but also to resist, "depart from me."
5. This will become your story at this retreat—
6. Pay attention to the new insights, the new awareness of yourself, of Christ, and of your new commitments.
7. Write them down as they come to you.

3:00 P.M.   BREAK

Session 2: You Are Loved Just As You Are
    3:45 P.M.   **Total Group**

(5 minutes)   Hymn: "O Love That Wilt Not Let Me Go"
(10 minutes)   **Story-telling:**

TIME	ACTIVITY	NOTES

The Story of the Prodigal Father
(Luke 15:1-11)

(10 minutes) **Alone Time**

Write whatever comes to your mind
as you reflect on the story.

(5 minutes) Lift your writing to God as a prayer.

4:15 P.M. **Small Groups**

Share your responses to the story.

Allow persons to self-select
groups. Use the same groups
throughout the retreat.

Groups may be six to seven if
work group settings indicate
larger groups than four.

5:00 P.M. BREAK

5:30 P.M. **Dinner**

Session 3: From Unfreedom into Freedom,
From Darkness into Light, From Sin to Salvation

7:30 P.M. **Total Group**

Hymn: "O Love That Wilt Not Let
Me Go"

Assignment:

"Re-membering" Our Own Journey

Construct the journey of your past
religious experience by identifying
and jotting down your responses to
the following questions:

1. At what point were you most
   aware of God in your life?

2. What was perhaps the most
   serious commitment you ever
   made to God?

3. At what points in your life has
   God seemed most near?

4. At what points in your life has
   God seemed farthest away?

Note: For your response, jot down:
What were the circumstances?
Who were the important persons
   in the circumstances?

TIME	ACTIVITY	NOTES
	When was it and *where* were you? *Why* is it important to you now? *How* is it important to you now?	
7:45 P.M.	Move to Small Groups	
8:10 P.M. (20 minutes)	**Alone Time** Reflect upon and jot down your responses to the questions.	
(45 minutes)	Share your responses to the questions.	
9:15 P.M.	**Dismiss to Refreshments**	

SECOND DAY

TIME	ACTIVITY	NOTES
7:45 A.M.	**Breakfast**	
8:30 A.M.	**Total Group** **Opening Worship** Psalm 139 Hymn: "Search me, O God" Prayer: The Lord's Prayer **Story-telling:** The Story of Zacchaeus (Luke 19:1-10)	
9:00 A.M.	**Alone Time**	
(10 minutes)	Prayerfully meditate upon the story and write whatever comes to your mind.	
(5 minutes)	Lift your writing to God as a prayer.	
9:15 A.M.	**Alone Time**	
(40 minutes)	Take an honest look at your spiritual life. Take ten minutes to find your "place," then spend thirty minutes working alone and in silence. In prayerfulness and honesty, reflect over your entire retreat experience—all you have heard, said, done, felt—and write your responses to the following:	

TIME	ACTIVITY	NOTES

1. What is the *true*, present condition of my own spiritual life and of my ministry?

2. *Truthfully*, what are the blockages/hindrances to my having a more vital life in Christ and a more satisfying, effective ministry?

3. What *actually* hinders me from taking concrete steps to reduce these blockages/hindrances?

4. What help do I need from others to take these steps? Who are these others?

9:55 A.M.   Move to Small Groups

10:15 A.M.   **Group Discussion of Private Responses to the Questions**

11:30 A.M.   BREAK

12:00 noon   **Lunch**
The break period after lunch is for persons to use as they wish—quiet reflection, exercise, serious conversation, recreation.

3:00 P.M.   **Total Group**
Lecture:
"The journey I have taken, and how I am endeavoring to keep Christ alive in my own experience."

This talk should be given by a significant leader, one who is respected for efforts to maintain a vital spirituality.

3:40 P.M.   **Alone Time**
Personal reflection on your own autobiography, as you have been developing it here at the retreat.

(20 minutes)   **Assignment:**
Ponder all that you have written, said, and experienced so far in the retreat regarding your own personal spirituality and the quality of your ministry in order to:

1. *Identify* the patterns of behavior which serve to strengthen/weaken your spiritual life and the effects of your ministry.

TIME	ACTIVITY	NOTES

2. *Consider* what God thinks about these characteristics of your personal spiritual life and your ministry.

3. *Reflect* again upon the question: "What steps might I take even now to reduce the blockages/hindrances to my spiritual growth and to a more effective, satisfying ministry?

Then—

(5 minutes)   Write a letter (a prayer) to God in two brief paragraphs regarding:

1. What I have experienced and learned about myself in the retreat.
2. What I intend to do about those learnings.

Then—

(5 minutes)   Write a letter (a meditation) from God to you about how God seems to be responding to your letter.

4:10 P.M.   **Small Groups**
Share your responses to the assignment.

5:15 P.M.   **Dinner**

7:00 P.M.   **Total Group**
Hymn: "Make Me a Captive, Lord"
General discussion of the afternoon experience. Questions and responses.

Session 4: Group Discernment Regarding Our Life and Ministry Together

7:30 P.M.   **Living in Covenant Community**
Plan for follow-up to this retreat.

NOTES: See page 74 for plan. Distribute copies of plan to each retreatant.

8:00 P.M.   Move to Small Groups

8:20 P.M.   **Small Groups**
Discuss "plan" in light of your own felt need and interest

TIME	ACTIVITY	NOTES

and
prepare a written response to the
plan, sharing strengths/weaknesses,
your group's suggestions to
strengthen plan.

9:30 P.M. **Evening prayers** in the small group.

THIRD DAY

7:30 A.M.

Bible Study:
Feeding the five thousand (Mark
6:33-44)

Alone and in silence, prayerfully
meditate upon the poetic symbols
and imagery of this story for your
own ministry and jot your insights
into the following questions:

1. What word, phrase, or symbol
   seems to be speaking most clearly
   to me about my own attitude toward my ministry?

   What is it saying to me about myself and my ministry?

2. Who is the "crowd" that I am trying to send away? Why am I doing
   this?

3. What do the two fish and five
   loaves represent in my own life
   and ministry?

4. What new vision of God's kingdom is God giving me in these
   days?

5. What does God seem to be saying
   to me about my/our ministry,
   even now?

8:00 A.M. **Breakfast**

8:30 A.M. **Total Group**
Psalm 91
Hymn: "How Great Thou Art"
Prayer
Lecture:
  The interrelationship of our spir-
  ituality to our professional minis-
  try and to our life together (as seen
  in Mark 6:33-44)

For resource, see Henri
Nouwen, *The Living Reminder*
(New York: The Seabury Press,
1981).

68

TIME	ACTIVITY	NOTES

9:00 A.M.   **Group reports** of responses to the "plan"
Brief discussion of the "plan" and responses

It will be necessary to have each group select a "reporter."

9:30 A.M.   Move to small groups

9:45 A.M.   **Small Group:**
Discerning the will of God for our personal and our communal lives and ministries.

(10 minutes)   Period of quiet prayer and reflection seeking the mind of God regarding
Your secret life

Psalm 139:23-24 (RSV)
Search me, O God, and know my heart!
Try me and know my thoughts!
And see if there be any wicked way in me,
and lead me in the everlasting way.

Questions for prayerful reflection:
1. When you search deep into my secret life, O Lord, what do you see?
2. What is the *true condition* of my inner, secret self?

(20 minutes)   Open discussion of what God seems to be saying to us about our personal lives.

(10 minutes)   Period of quiet prayer and reflection seeking the mind of God regarding
Your life in Christ

Ephesians 3:14-19 (RSV)
For this reason I bow my knees before the Father, from whom every family in heaven and on earth is named, that according to the riches of his glory he may grant you to be strengthened with might through his Spirit in the inner man, and that Christ may dwell in your heart through faith; that you, being rooted and grounded in love, may have power to comprehend with

TIME	ACTIVITY	NOTES

all the saints what is the breadth and length and height and depth, and to know the love of Christ which surpasses knowledge, that you may be filled with all the fulness of God.

Continued in the afternoon session.

Question for prayerful reflection:
What in particular, O Lord, who created the universe, do you want to say to me about my life and ministry, even now?

(20 minutes) Open discussion of what God seems to be saying to us about our public lives and ministries

(10 minutes) Period of quiet prayer and reflection seeking the mind of God regarding *Your life together* as (name of group)

Matthew 18:19–20 (RSV)
Again, I say to you, if two of you agree on earth about anything they ask, it will be done for them by my Father in heaven. For where two or three come together in my name, there am I in the midst of them.

James 5:16 (RSV)
Therefore confess your sins to one another, and pray for one another, that you may be healed. The prayer of a righteous man has great power in its effects.

Questions for prayerful reflection:
1. What in particular, O Lord who created the universe, do you want us (name of group) to do about our collective life and ministry, even now?
2. How do you want me to help make this happen?

(50 minutes) Open discussion of our findings, their implications for our personal lives and our community as (name of group)
and, finally, the question:
Is God asking us as a group to give

TIME	ACTIVITY	NOTES
	ourselves in any way to the "plan" or some variation of it?	
(5 minutes)	**Concluding prayer of thanksgiving** for the gift of God's discernment	
11:50 A.M.	BREAK	
12:00 Noon	**Lunch**	
1:15 P.M.	**Total Group** Reports from groups concerning their prayerful search for God's will for their group, and the entire community of (name of group). Group decision regarding next step on the "plan." Celebration of thanksgiving for the Spirit of God and the mind of God given to us.	
1:45 P.M.	**Total Group** Heading into the headwinds of our everyday responsibilities and realities.	See next page for design.
2:50 P.M.	**Closing Worship** Homily (Mal. 3:16–17) Eucharist	

Comments about the Assignments in the Design

1. Due to the nature of the assignments, it is necessary to print the entire design for each retreatant.
2. The "plan" must be well–prepared and printed so that each retreatant has a copy for personal and group study.
3. You may want to distribute the "plan" to the group prior to the retreat so that they may familiarize themselves with it.

A RETREAT CONCLUSION

Holding on to Our New State of Consciousness as We Turn into the Headwinds

(5 minutes)

The feeding of the five thousand gave the disciples a new glimpse of Jesus' vision of the kingdom and of their role in making it come true. For a few moments they gained a new state of consciousness that allowed them to enter into a new reality—where five loaves and two fish can indeed feed five thousand.

Here in this retreat each of us has no doubt experienced shifts in our own consciousness—we have gained new perspectives, new ideas, and new experiences. We have made new commitments regarding our private lives with Christ and about the service we will do in his name.

Now as we begin to move from this retreat back into our various worlds think about the many shifts of consciousness you have had here—the new insights, ideas, and discoveries, and the commitments you have made.

Find a comfortable place anywhere within the hearing of my voice and spend twenty minutes reflecting upon the entire retreat experience. Read through your notes, recall your conversations, scan the scripture passages. Then write down the new states of consciousness which have come to you.

——— 20 minutes of silence ———

Mark 6:45-52

Immediately after the experience of feeding the five thousand a most interesting thing happened. Jesus sent the disciples into the sea in their little boat while he went away to the mountain to pray.

Soon a fierce storm swept over the sea. The headwinds coming upon them threatened to tear their boat apart and destroy them all. But Jesus saw them and came to them—but when they saw him, they cried out in fear, believing it was a ghost.

What had happened here? Why didn't they recognize Christ?

In the moment of the miracle of feeding the five thousand the disciples had experienced the mind of Christ; they had experienced a new glimpse into his vision of the kingdom. They had entered a new state of consciousness that allowed them to participate in the miracle.

But here in the storm, they got all caught up in the headwinds. They forgot all about their new state of consciousness—and took on their former state of being.

So when Christ came again they didn't think he was real. They thought he was a ghost. So Mark says in verse 52. They hadn't integrated the miracle time into their own everyday experience. The vision had not yet become their vision. They did not hold on to their new state of consciousness.

Look at Peter in the storm. When he stepped out of the boat it was as if the wind was now at his back, moving him along rapidly toward Christ.

Sometimes we will feel the winds at our backs—moving us faster than we want. Sometimes the speed with which we move toward God frightens us, and we become timid and begin to sink.

In a little while we will leave this "miracle" place and head into the headwinds of our daily responsibilities and realities. What are the headwinds you will be facing? And what does God want you to do about those?

Take twenty minutes in silence to think about the headwinds into which you will soon go. Write them down. Then prayerfully lift each one of them to God. Ask God what you might do about them, and ask how you might keep holding on to your new state of consciousness in the midst of them. Write down the ideas which come to you. Receive them as the word of God for you.

——— 20 minutes of silence ———

(5 minutes)
Now pair up with another person and spend fifteen minutes talking about the new ideas, commitments, states of consciousness—and the headwinds—and what you plan to do about them when you go home.

——— 15 minutes of sharing time ———

(This concluding retreat experience was prepared by Bruce R. Ough. We are grateful for his permission to include it here.)

COVENANT PLAN

In a pressure-packed age like today, it is not unusual for persons to enter "the winter of the soul." Clergypersons are no exception. In fact, ministers can give so much without replenishment that they become barren.

The Covenant Plan has been designed to provide a wellspring of living water for those desiring spiritual replenishment. The plan is in two parts: 1) the present retreat and 2) a five-month commitment plan.

In the second part of the plan you are asked to become a member of a covenant group. To do so will involve a commitment on your part. The following information and suggestions may help you make your covenant.

Structure and Scope

Covenant groups should be formed so that each person can become a part of a group within reasonable traveling distance. Each group will have six–to–ten members. Some of the features of this group will be that:
- each member covenants with the other members.
- the group will meet regularly for five months.
- the group will not meet unless everyone can be present.
- the group will meet in a place conducive to renewal for all members.
- the group will attend the concluding one-day retreat.
- each member will pray for the other members.

Basic Plan (Minimal Requirements)

There is a basic plan which all groups should try to follow. Some groups may wish to do more, but the following suggestions should be minimal:
- Meet once a month as a covenant group.
- Read Life Together by Dietrich Bonhoeffer.
- Practice daily disciplines of prayer and meditation for one hour (Monday through Friday).[2]
- Read and meditate on the daily assigned scripture selections (Monday through Friday).
- Pray daily for the others in your covenant group.
- Keep a daily journal to record your thoughts, feelings, and experiences (Monday through Friday).
- Share periodic progress reports with state/city office, if one exists.

Options for the Basic Plan

For those desiring to do more, you may want to consider some of these suggestions or you may have your own suggestions. Remember, the whole covenant group needs to adopt them.
- Meet twice a month.
- Read and use Celebration of Discipline by Richard Foster as the content of discussion for the bi-weekly meetings (see Bibliography).
- Read Spirituality for Ministry by Urban T. Holmes (see Bibliography).
- Discuss the meaning of ministry for yourself and for a minister of your denomination.
- Schedule and plan a one-day retreat for the covenant group.

Process

What needs to happen at the retreat to insure completion of the plan:
• Choose options desired in addition to the basic plan.
• Each person covenants to specific accountabilities.
• When your group meets, select a coordinator, who will remain in that position for the full five months. However, two people may want to share this responsibility.
• The coordinator will make arrangements for the monthly meetings, mail reminders, (if any), and insure monthly leadership for each meeting.
• Determine the calendar for the five months—dates, times, places.
• Reserve a date for the concluding one-day retreat for the Covenant Plan meeting. This date will be suggested at this retreat.

Possible Places to Meet

Each covenant group is urged to give careful thought to where the group will meet monthly. The place should be conducive to renewal. You need to be away from interruptions and in a place where communication can flow easily.

For those groups wanting to have a one-day retreat, the following sites are suggested for your consideration. You may want to note some possible choices under each heading.

• State parks • Denominational retreat sites • Catholic Retreat Houses • Other centers

Journey in Renewal

OUR COVENANT

After careful consideration and in common pursuit of the renewal of our spiritual lives, we hereby covenant with one another to do the following:

DATE _____

SIGNED: _____   _____

             _____   _____

             _____   _____

             _____   _____

4.

The Personally Guided Retreat

With the exciting renewal of the retreat movement in so many of our Christian churches over the past few years, there has been an increasing interest in, and a continuing demand for, more opportunities to take part in a "directed" or a "personally guided" retreat.

The overwhelming popularity of this style of contemplative experience is due in no small part to the sharpened sense of personal awareness that the people of God are experiencing—a deep yearning for a more felt knowledge of God, a real hunger for a more intimate relationship with the living God. This inner, Spirit-led stirring has led many people over the past years to experience a personally guided prayer retreat. Such retreats are both an invitation to take more seriously our inner life and a time of renewal of our commitment to the gospel values of the Christian life.

The purpose of this chapter, then, is to offer some reflections and suggestions for those drawn to make this manner of reflective retreat. It will also afford some insight into the role of the retreat guide.

THE RETREAT DYNAMIC

A guided retreat is a special opportunity to open ourselves to the inner movements of the Holy Spirit in extended periods of personal prayer. It is a time to slow down, to relax in the quiet of a contemplative setting, and to become aware of God's presence and action more intensely than is normally possible in the work-a-day world. In order to allow God to be the prime director in this retreat, the emphasis is put not on conferences or talks given to the retreatants but on the personal life and individual prayer experiences of each retreatant.

The focus thus shifts from listening to the words of others to listening to the *inner word* that God speaks to the praying person's heart. Much unstructured free time allows the retreatants to relax enough interiorly to begin paying attention to their own unique inspirations and to get in touch with the "ups and downs" of their own personal story—the various sentiments, feelings, thoughts, and movements that go deep within our inner selves.

This style of personalized retreat provides enough silence, quiet space and inner room for retreatants to know and reflect upon the ways of God in their own particular lives, to come to deeper insights, and to experience closer ties to Jesus and a more affirmed place in his saving love. The moments of prayer can be uplifting and refreshing and can renew a long-term love relationship with God and with others. It can also be a time of growth and challenge to live the life of Christian discipleship with more conviction in faith and more commitment in love and loyalty.

Even the few sessions that are held with the group during a personally guided retreat tend to be marked by a certain simplicity and clarity. This prevents the minds of retreatants from being overcrowded with new ideas and insights or their hearts from being overwhelmed by the retreat guide's own personal thoughts and emotions.

The chief function of the retreat guide is to help an individual to *be real before God* and to *let God be real* for that individual. This guiding helper encourages the person to spend time alone with God in some form of contemplative and reflective prayer, listening to the inner stirrings of the Spirit. The retreatants meet individually once or twice a day with the guide in order to share what has been brought to their attention during the time of quiet prayerfulness. This is a time each day to talk over the "ups and downs" of one's life story as it comes to consciousness; a time to seek the director's affirming companionship as well as to clarify what has really happened during the day; a time to ask for feedback, challenge, and helps to "discern" better where one is being led. Finally, it is a time to dialogue about further materials for prayer and reflection and to receive suggestions for the next day's contemplation.

Hopefully, the retreatant will discover his/her own daily rhythm of rest, reflection, relaxation, and prayer in a context of peace and solitude. The important elements in the ingredients for this type of retreat experience are a generous and open heart, a real desire to meet God in our lives, an innate willingness to be available in gentle listening, and a real intent to cooperate with every grace God will send.

THE RETREATANT

Since the focus of a personally guided retreat is on the individual's experiences of what happens in his/her life of prayer, this form of retreat seems best suited for those who desire to be apart, to spend some time in solitude, to invest energy in contemplative reflection and quiet prayer. Some may come feeling that they have neglected their spiritual lives, that prayer has become routine and dull, that Christian life has lost some of its initial challenge. In these times, the Spirit has stirred up many who were apathetic and has led them to seek out spiritual help, to take steps to renew their devotional practices, to dialogue more seriously with another about the implications of the faith for modern times, and simply to desire "more" for their lives.

The desire to pray and a hunger for a deeper relationship with God in a world of hunger, injustice, poverty, war, greed, and power-grabbing have led many to find the personally guided retreat to be an important stage in their recommitment to the Christian life. The person who comes to a directed retreat should have the ability and willingness to dialogue with a director, to carry on a one-on-one conversation about the inner movements, the dark and light moments of his or her life. It is here that God will be encountered and shared. This kind of trust and intimacy with another can be difficult at times, particularly if this is a new experience for the retreatant. Entrusting ourselves to a guide can be a risky business (as can trusting ourselves to God). Our prayer and personal life experiences are secret and deeply personal affairs. We can all be reluctant to share what goes on in our hearts when we stand before God in prayer. "Am I really praying, or is it talking to myself using God-language?" "Is my life significant enough to share it with another, since it seems to have no clear distinction?" "How well-founded is my Christian commitment to Jesus? Can it encompass some serious doubts about religious values?" These and like questions, doubts, fears, and hesitations can easily come to our awareness.

Yet in spite of all these inner uncertainties, the retreatant should realize that there are no set, preconceived expectations that must be met. The retreat guide has no fixed game plan that has to be followed, no predetermined results that have to be achieved. When we seek to "be real before the Lord," to be honest and open in time of quiet prayer, telling the Lord the whole story (Mark 5:33), letting God be revealed deep in the movements of our heart, then *whatever results from that recognized and felt experience* is God's good news. The result can be an intense experience of uplifting peace, a quiet joy, a sense that all is well. It can also be a period of dryness and darkness. It may be a time of wrestling with our "shadow" or celebrating our freedom.

Individuals who have never prayed quietly this way are often surprised to find that their contemplative capacity is rich and deep and has never been given the chance to develop and grow. During the sessions with the retreat director, the individual often comes to a deeper realization that God has been indeed working on his/her behalf.

The prayer-dialogue with God continues in the dialogue with the guide. One feeds the other. Many retreatants begin to experience the Living God both within the times set aside for formal prayer and, more startlingly, during the times of informal chatting with the director. The God of freedom is not bound by our structures and schedules. God even encounters us in sleep, rest, and times of relaxation (Ps. 127:2). This is why the whole context of the personally guided retreat is contemplative and geared to meet God.

THE RETREAT GUIDE

It goes without saying that the real Guide, the primary Director, in this form of retreat is, of course, the Holy Spirit, who leads the retreatant deep from within. The human retreat director has the important role of facilitator of that primal relationship between the retreatant and God. The guide seeks to foster the prayer initiatives of the individual retreatant, to direct the person to dialogue with God in loving response, and to help in uncovering the mystery of God in that unique person's life.

The retreat director is neither a teacher nor a preacher of the gospel. He or she imposes no set form of prayer, no preachments, no teachings on the "right" way to carry out directions. The personally guided retreat is not a classroom so much as a "school of prayer" and a time of discovering God in the intimacy of personal dialogue. Instead of talking learnedly about the Bible, the journey to God, or the ways of perfection, the guide's job is to point the individual on retreat to a personal experience of a personal, loving God. The retreat director will make needed suggestions for daily prayer periods, but these are only proposals, only a framework of scriptural texts so that God may speak through the Word directly to the heart of the retreatant at prayer. A list of typical texts will be included at the end of this chapter.

The daily session with the retreat guide centers around the prayer experiences of the day, those that have happened during the in–between, informal times. This is the area of spiritual movement and enlightenment by God's Spirit. The guide seeks to listen attentively to the "story," helping with empathy so that the retreatant can more clearly express his/her reactions and responses, own them more personally, and attempt to discern the meaning and significance of their occurrence at this time.

The role of the director is one of companionship and trusting accompaniment. Such a role is carried out in honesty and openness when the guide finds the sharing an opportunity for *affirmation* of the individual's experience of God. It is a time for underlining for retreatants the fact that something good has come for that person in their relationship with God. The retreat director is called upon at times to give feedback. It can be a time of *challenge* for the retreatant, a call to look more deeply at things that have happened, to delve into one's experiences of "light" or "darkness" more intently so as to discover hidden meanings and spirited directions. Finally, the retreat guide knows when to step back and let God deal directly with the retreatant. The guide must have complete respect for the grace of God and for the complete freedom of the praying person to be led by that grace without interference. This personal separation informs the individual on retreat that the guide is neither a guru nor a wise old seer, but a companion on the way whose support and encouragement is ever available for discerning God's leadings.

SUMMARY

The personally guided or "directed" retreat is a moment in a person's journey of the heart toward God. The setting finds a person at a particular point in his or her concrete pilgrimage, at a certain stage of growth and challenge, whether this be a time of pleasure or pain, consolation or desolation. Persons seeking a directed retreat experience may be seeking help in a critical life decision; struggling with serious personal or family problems; or facing the conflict and confusion of a loss, a death, a period of sickness, or lack of love in their private life and/or working conditions. Thus, the personally guided retreat cannot be divorced from the realities that make up an individual's everyday experience.

The retreat director agrees to walk with the retreatant during this time apart to aid in contemplative prayer, in articulating and discerning the alternating movements of the retreatant's inner life with God and others. Both need to be open to the actions of the Holy Spirit, to talk about personal feelings and intimate, deep desires, to discuss spiritual sensings and leadings of diverse spirits—hopes, fears, peace and turmoil, poverty, injustice, lack of love and sheer ecstasy, tranquil nights and conflicted days, the "ups and downs" of real human existence lived in the presence of God.

The manner in which the retreat director functions as spiritual guide to the retreatants is of major importance in a personally guided retreat. For that reason we have decided to include a brief word about the guide and guidance.

GUIDELINES FOR SPIRITUAL GUIDES

Terms clarified:
1. **Spiritual Guidance** (also called "Spiritual Direction," "Spiritual Advising," "Spiritual Help," "Spiritual Counseling").
   - Those means by which an individual becomes aware of the life of the Holy Spirit within himself or herself and is assisted in working out a response to this inner presence and its dynamic movements.
   - A kind of companionship, a walking along with, a time of being with another on the journey-of-faith, starting right where the person is.
   - An interpersonal situation where one individual (the guide) assists another (the retreatant) to develop and come to greater maturity in the life of the Spirit; that is, the life of faith, hope, and love.
   - Not a counseling or information-giving or therapeutic session, although this may occur at one time or another, but rather a "discernment" session wherein the two people, director and retreatant, seek to uncover the affective movements that make up their inner lives in order to find the Spirit and thus listen to the word of God to them here and now.

2. **Spiritual Guide** (Spiritual Director/Spiritual Advisor). The terms are interchangeable, but the word Guide better emphasizes the spiritual role as secondary to the real Director, the Holy Spirit.

   • An experienced, prayerful person who helps the retreatant to become more aware of the inner movements, the deep affectivity of the human heart, where the Spirit leads and inspires an individual to live more rooted in faith, hope, and love.

   • A caring, empathetic, listening presence.

   • An instrument and servant of the Lord who at different times is an understanding and supportive friend, a help to better self-understanding, an encouraging and at times a challenging companion. Someone who knows when to back off and let the Lord lead.

   • Spiritual guides are persons of faith who are aware of their own affective and inner experiences and who have a strong sense that God works in another's inner life. The guide is comfortable with silence and with waiting for another to speak. The guide has a faith that is biblically grounded and rooted in the church. A person who enjoys being with a wide variety of people, the guide is sensitive, patient, open and affirming, prayerful, compassionate, empathetic, and nonjudgemental. The guide understands that he or she is accountable to God (see 3 below).

3. **Accountability.** A spiritual guide should:

   • regularly receive spiritual direction himself or herself. Getting in touch with the movements of the Spirit in one's own personal life is essential in helping others to get in touch with the leadings of the Holy Spirit in their lives.

   • periodically, perhaps once every two to three months, receive some supervision in dealings with others as a spiritual helper. This could involve participating in "practicum" sessions run for a group of directors by an experienced spiritual guide acting as advising supervisor. These sessions can be a great help to the inexperienced director as well as to the more advanced guides.

   • take part in other upgrading activities, such as workshops on contemplative prayer, discernment, skills in the art of listening, and the dynamics of supervision.

COMPONENTS OF A PERSONALLY GUIDED RETREAT

A personally guided retreat incorporates the following basic components:

1. An *introductory session*, with all the persons together, to set the stage for the retreat.

2. A *daily group worship* with brief homily to present the theme the retreatants are to pray and reflect upon throughout the day and to announce the gift of grace the retreatant is to seek.

3. Much *unstructured time for solitude* in which each retreatant is encouraged to be real with him/herself and the Lord—to pray, meditate, journal, rest.

4. A daily time for each retreatant to meet in *private conference with the guide* (thirty to sixty minutes) to discuss what is being dealt with in the hours of solitude and what the Word is bringing to awareness and to receive help in discerning the movements of the Spirit in the experience.

This is also a time for the guide to expand upon the prayer theme, to be more helpful in guiding the retreatant's prayer and reflection, and to paint directions for the retreatant to seek more openly the gift of grace.

The guide may decide to meet privately with some retreatants twice a day. However, time constraints will not allow this to be the norm if there are more than three retreatants for each guide. Also, too much time spent with the guide will weaken the effects of solitude and contemplation.

Each of the following designs will:

1. present a general theme for the retreat,
2. suggest possible content for the opening session, and
3. give helps for the daily private conferences with each retreatant, from which can also be taken homily ideas for the daily worship sessions.

PERSONALLY GUIDED RETREAT DESIGN 1

Conditions Suggesting This Retreat Design:

Group Size: 1 to 5 per director

2. Type of Audience: General

3. Length of Retreat: 3 to 5 days

4. Note: The material outlined in this design can be adapted for any number of sessions and extended for a longer retreat by adding further scripture texts for prayer and contemplation.

Retreat Theme

"If you continue in my word,
   you are truly my disciples,
and you will know the truth,
   and the truth will make you free." (John 8:31-32, RSV)

Introductory Session

Introductions: The individuals in the retreat group are asked to tell others about themselves, where they come from, why they were drawn to this retreat, etc.

Setting the Stage: The guide (if only one) or each guide (if more than one) says a few words about one or more of the following topics:

• Prayer: This time of retreat is a special time of listening, making oneself available to the promptings of the Holy Spirit—a time for personal prayer, a time of receiving and responding to God's initiatives.

• Silence: This is also a time of quiet and peaceful recollecting, a time and space apart from the ordinary patterns of everyday life, a time for deep ponderings and relaxed, contemplative stillness.

• The role of the guide in this retreat:

   acts as spiritual helper and is available as companion and guide, conversing with the retreatant on whatever comes up during the quiet times;

   offers passages from scripture for the individual's ponderings and contemplation, the privileged places for encountering the Lord;

   helps the praying person discern the inner movements that occur during this extended time of involvement with God.

• Freedom: The retreat should be a time of greatest possible personal freedom, a time of unstructured availability. This freedom includes:

place, time, frequency of prayer times and methods of individual prayer;

possibility of making an initial choice of directors from the list of available guides, freedom to decide the length of the retreat itself and even the possibility of making a change in directors if necessary;

the nature of group experiences, including shared prayer sessions, preparation for times of worship, and voluntary participation in either "talked" or "quiet" mealtimes

• Community: Although a personally guided retreat is not a group experience as such, "community" is celebrated by achieving the smallest community possible. The trust relationship that develops between the director, the person on retreat, and the Holy Spirit is the bond. The director and retreatant, together with the loving God, make up a powerful community of sharing, trusting Christians.

Practical Details:

Be certain retreatants know the times for common meals and the places that are reserved for talking around the house.

Post the times and places for meetings with the retreat directors. Tell retreatants the possibilities for walks and/or other exercise. (Be sure that there *is* some place for exercise.)

Daily Group Worship

The daily worship session can be centered on the day's theme, which will be used to guide the private conversations with the retreatant. Generally the daily worship will be brief and not allow for dialogue. It may include such elements as:

•a celebration of the Word: a reading from the Bible and perhaps a very brief homily

•a time set aside after the reading for some quiet, a time for brief shared prayer together

•a celebration of the Lord's Supper or an agape meal with appropriate hymns and music

Daily Individual Sessions

When meeting with the individual retreatants, the guide may use some of the suggestions given below. *Note:* Since each person is unique, it is clear that a great deal of adaptation will occur even within this very free outline.

Process

Take each of the phrases from John's text as they are divided in the following pages. Each day dialogue with the retreatant over the meaning and significance as applied to their lives and experiences in this retreat.

Suggest that the individual pray over some of the materials and texts suggested in the interview.

FIRST DAY

Individual Sessions (and theme for community worship)

"If you continue": This opening phrase points out the basic and essential condition of this retreat—the "if," the individual's personal investment, his/her responsibility to stay with and correspond with the leading graces of God's inspired word. This "if" involves:

1. a certain *generosity* of heart, an openness to whatever God will reveal during this time apart, and the trust that something will happen if we puts our faith in the workings of the Holy Spirit;

2. the *initial desire* to meet God; a hunger for "more" in our relationship with God; a need to be apart and ponder the direction of our lives and reflect on our Christian commitment;

3. an ability to be *quiet*, to relax in the solitude that will be provided; to involve ourselves in inner listening so that real prayer can happen, so that the contemplative attitude can come alive in our whole being, to have a silent heart;

4. a trust in the *process* of "direction," given both by the inner workings of the Spirit and in the daily dialogue with the retreat guide so that real spiritual growth can occur and the relationship with God can deepen and call us forth to a richer Christian life in the world.

In my word: This phrase underlines the power of God's presence in the Word; it will be the sacred scripture that will occupy most of the quiet periods of the retreatant's prayer, abiding in, being nurtured by, and encountering the living God within the Word. This is a time to recall the dynamism proclaimed in Isaiah 55:10-11 (NASB):

> As the rain and snow come down from heaven
> And do not return there without watering the earth,
> And making it bear and sprout,
> And furnishing seed to the sower and bread to the eater; So shall My word that goes forth from my mouth;
> It shall not return to Me empty, without accomplishing what I desire,
> And without succeeding in the matter for which I sent it.

God's word comes to us in a wide variety of ways, from different sources and diverse circumstances. As Maxie Dunnam wrote in *Alive in Christ:*

> Bushes are often aflame all around us, but we fail to see. God is persistently speaking though we allow more clamorous noises to drown out "his still small voice." I am learning slowly to stay alert, to look and to listen, for the Lord's reminder that the ground on which I stand is holy and I need to take off my shoes for a while and give attention to what is communicated.[1]

Some considerations for the first periods of contemplative solitude and prayer on the Word of God:
- The Word that comes to us in and through the external, objective world of *created reality:* the works of God in nature and creation, all the things that touch our five senses—sky and clouds; rain and sunlight; cool breezes and warm winds; the sea and all its power, depth, and beauty, its lifegiving waters, and its ability to destroy; the earth we live on; soil and seed; rock and forest; flower and shrub. Reflect on the immense wonder that is *creation* (Ps. 104; Wisd. of Sol. 12; Job 38–39).
- The Word that comes to us in and through God's having shared *creative powers* with humankind. Reflect on the world of art and architecture, music and drama, poetry and literature, sculpture and painting, dance and singing, story-telling and the creative imagination! Ponder some of the great poetry of the Bible: The Song of Solomon; Psalms 23 and 139; the Magnificat (Luke 1:46-55), and hymns in Philippians 2:5-11; Ephesians 1:3-14; and 1 Corinthians 13:1-13. Suggest some readings from the great religious poetry in Christian literature!
- The Word that God speaks to us in and within our own life experience. Consider the fabric of our own "story," the manifold traces of God's love and grace—the shared blessings and gifts that are ours and are often left forgotten; the talented people; the gracious friends; the caring individuals, old and young, near and far, that have touched our lives; the moments of healing and uplift; the times that were hard but gotten through; the special presence of God (cf. Ps. 139; Isa. 42:43; Matt. 6:25-34; Mark 5:25-34; Luke 15).
- The Word that God speaks to us through the inspired works of the biblical accounts. Ponder the ongoing story of God's revealing love for the chosen people; the final and fullest Word spoken in the life, ministry, death, and resurrection of Jesus; the continuing revelation to us in our lives today of that same Word (cf. Heb. 1:1 ff.; John 1; 1 John 1).

SECOND DAY

Individual Sessions (and theme for community worship)

"You are truly my disciples": The retreatant is reminded from pondering this segment of John's text that we are all called to be "followers of Jesus," to be in discipleship. Being in discipleship involves:
- *a process of growth*—learning, listening, being taught in the school of Jesus Christ. It is a time to bury the seed of Jesus' life and teachings deep in our hearts and psyches, a time to reroot our priorities

into those of Jesus, a time to be led and challenged by the indwelling Spirit to live a more authentic Christian life, a time to re–examine our vital commitments, a time to seek and find, to ask and receive from the Lord (cf. Rev. 3:20-21; John 15:1-27; Mark 8:27-33; Luke 5:1-11).

• *praying in the Spirit*, as Paul reminds us in Romans 8:26-27 (RSV):

> Likewise the Spirit helps us in all our weakness; for we do not know how to pray as we ought, but the Spirit intercedes for us with sighs too deep for words. And he who searches the hearts . . . knows what is the mind of the Spirit, because the Spirit intercedes for the saints according to the will of God.

• *the journey* to meet Jesus along the way of life and responding to his invitation to *metanoia*, a change of heart, that inner conversion that purifies the Christian commitment to follow Jesus. In Luke 19:1-10 note three elements that make up the religious experience that can be ours: a dynamic set of movements, Christian discipleship, and the conversion process.

1. *A dynamic set of movements:* each moving toward the other, the divine initiative and the human response!

   Zacchaeus moves with an initial desire to *"see"* Jesus, to experience in some way the person of Jesus that he has heard about (faith comes from hearing). This movement illustrates what a true disciple seeks: greater knowledge of and a deeper meeting with the journeying Lord along the way.

   Jesus is already on the way; he has begun his movement without any advance warning to the individuals on the route. No one knows where, when, or how often he will stop to engage bystanders; he is certain, however, to pass our way. The certainty of our faith is that God will always take the initiative. God's grace draws us toward our creator.

   The inner movement of the human heart will reach out, for our hearts were made for God and they will not rest until they rest in God. It may be absolutely necessary, however, to do all that we can to cooperate in that meeting: choose a place that will give some perspective, a place apart, a tree to perch on. Find a time to get ready to prepare the soil of the heart, to get away from, up, and above the noise of the crowd, to create that necessary inner space so that we can truly let the Lord into our house!

2. *Christian discipleship:* a meeting with a difference, the process of discovering and being discovered!

   Something was missing in the "rich life" of Zacchaeus. Luke introduces him as a person with a few strikes against him; he has a reputation among his own folk that is not the best. He is not trustworthy as a Jew because he deals with the Romans and seemingly makes money for himself out of that arrangement.

   That Zacchaeus in his own person is portrayed as being "small of stature" not only tells us about his physical stature but also hints at his psychological and/or spiritual stature. He is far from being a perfect specimen, either of body or of soul. But he does want something *more* than what he has, and he wants it so badly that he has to overcome some very serious obstacles.

   Zacchaeus has to take the necessary steps to overcome the initial obstacle of the crowd's size and number; he then has to overcome their ridicule as he "climbs a tree"—obviously an embarrassing situation. He finally has to endure the constant carping criticism before, during, and after the tree positioning. But the risks taken prove worthwhile!

   Something was happening in Jesus' heart as he moved to the happy encounter with Zacchaeus; he too was "seeing," he too was looking deeply, contemplating the crowd as he approached the city. His eyes met those of the man in the tree. His words communicate a sense of urgency and need to be with Zacchaeus. Is it possible that Jesus has needs for companionship and at-homeness with others? Taste his words here, "Make haste and come down; for I must stay at your house today" (19:5, RSV).

Note the use of the proper name, so characteristic of biblical "possessiveness," and the use of the house, the personal home of Zacchaeus and the whole house of Israel—a reminder of Jesus' concern for universal salvation. Also note that the time together is private, intimate, and a wordless sharing (in the context of a meal).

There is a conflict of moods here, an exchange of "spirits." The crowd murmurs disapproval, Zacchaeus exults, and Jesus seems bold and forthright. Zacchaeus rejoices and has a deep inner conversion of heart (metanoia), admitting his past failures and sins and now accepting the grace of really being "at-home" with himself and the Lord, despite his isolation by the crowd. Again we experience that Jesus comes to us where we live and loves us just as we are.

3. *The Conversion process*

Every encounter with Jesus changes the individual Christian in some way or other; the "being with Jesus in discipleship" will make demands on us: a deeper commitment in faith to the gospel values, a letting go more and more of our personal fears and doubts. It will often entail a simplification of lifestyle and a reaffirmation of the need for prayer and fasting. It will stir up in us the practice of *spiritual disciplines* that foster and nourish the religious experience of having met Jesus.

THIRD DAY
Individual Sessions (and theme for community worship)

Learning the truth that sets one free: "Now the Lord is the Spirit, and where the Spirit of the Lord is, there is true freedom" (2 Cor. 3:17, RSV).

The fundamental purpose of every form of retreat in this manual, whether dialogic, preached, guided, or privately made, has as its ultimate goal the inner freedom of the Christian heart.

The retreatant is led in prayer to discover anew God's immense availability, God's ever-abiding love, the profound gift of the Holy Spirit within the life and actions of the Christian heart. Pondering the *promises* that Jesus made to his disciples in the upper room before his death and accepting the fact that they have been fulfilled and are now being experienced in each individual life will finally bring us to grow in the truth and to be set free to love and serve God and humankind.

The spirit of the risen Jesus is alive and well, forming the body of Christ, liberating the heart of each Christian from its strictures and fears (1 Cor. 12-14 / Rom. 12:3-8; Eph. 4:7-16 / 1 Pet. 4:10; Col. 1:27 / 1 Cor. 2:10-13).

The freeing promises of Jesus have been fulfilled; the experience of Pentecost continues in the church, and the Holy Spirit is ours forever:

> John 14:15-17—our freely given guest
> John 14:25-27—our teacher and rememberer
> John 15:26-27—our companion and witness
> John 16:7-11—our judge and truth-giver
> John 16:13-15—our guide and our hope

Note: Sessions two and three may each be divided into two segments if the guide is meeting with the retreatant twice each day or if the retreat is four or five days in length rather than three days.

PERSONALLY GUIDED RETREAT DESIGN 2

Conditions Suggesting This Design:

1. **Group Size:**   1 to 5 per director
2. **Type of Audience:**   General
3. **Length of Retreat:**   3 to 5 days
4. **Note:** Design 1 is based on a textual theme which is used to guide the retreatants' contemplation throughout the entire retreat. Design 2 suggests another way to approach the personally guided retreat; that is, to choose a *topical theme* for each day. The topics are selected to provide a progression in the retreatants' contemplation.

FIRST DAY
Introductory Session
Introductions: The retreatants are invited at the first group session to introduce themselves very briefly and to say a few words about where they have come from and what they are seeking in this retreat. They may be seeking rest and relaxation, a time alone, some opportunities to deepen their prayer life, a chance to talk to an experienced guide about the spiritual experiences they have been going through, or just the time to breathe more freely and rest more securely in the life of faith that is theirs.

Setting the Stage
"You created my inmost being" (Ps. 139:13, NIV).
At the very start of these quiet days of prayer persons on retreat need to be encouraged to *relax*, to be themselves before God, and to take as much time to slow down and get settled as they need. It might be good simply to "chat" with retreatants about life in general and their life stories in particular.

The Word of God as it is found in each person's own "story" is an excellent way to draw the person into contemplative prayer: A LOVING LOOK AT THE "REAL." No haste, no great demands made on what to remember . . . just letting the individual come up with what comes up. Pondering a psalm like Psalm 139 may be a help. Some have found concentrating on the beauties of nature all around them a way into prayer, slowly using their five senses as they wander around the retreat house setting.

The Day's Theme for Contemplation

God is in my story:
• God provides my basic needs (Matt. 6:25-34).
• God accomplishes great things for and through me (Luke 1:46-55).
• Nothing can separate me from God and the love of God (Rom. 8:26-38).

The Grace which we Seek throughout the Day

At this point in the retreat we ask for a simple yet deep awareness of and trust in the presence of God in our lives.

Individual Sessions

When meeting with the individual retreatants, the guide will assist the person to go more deeply into the day's theme as it is being experienced in his or her own story. In order to allow retreatants to reflect on their relationship with God, some of the following background questions might be used to stimulate conversation. Abandon this list, however, when it becomes too stilted or overly structured in the dialogue with the retreatant.

1. How do you picture God; what *image* do you bear in your prayer and devotions?
2. How do you approach God? With what kind of feelings?
3. How would you describe your faith relationship to God? Is it friendly?
4. In what ways do you pray? Do you have any creative approaches that need to be underlined and affirmed?
5. What practical effects does your relationship with God have on your daily life? Does faith make a difference?
6. How do you define your faith? Does what you believe and practice flow from your own free choice, or is it simply what others have told you to believe and do?

SECOND DAY
Community Worship
The Day's Theme for Contemplation

God is the Creator and Giver of Life.
• In today's prayer encourage the retreatant to reflect further upon his or her life as LIFE and as GIFT from God. Ask individuals to look at the *people* and the *places* that have brought goodness to them and have enriched their lives. How have they experienced the beauty, wonder, and amazement of God's caring love? (Cf. Ps. 139; Gen. 1:26-28, 2-7; John 10:10-29.)

Note: See the suggestions for Daily Group Worship, Retreat Design No. 1, page 83.

The Grace which we Seek throughout the Day
• That we experience a growing sense of wonder, joy, and utter amazement that God has loved us and gifted us with so many people, gifts, and situations that I have taken for granted.

Individual Sessions

As helps to allow the retreatants to deepen their life of gratitude for God's care and love and God's continual act of blessing and gift-giving, some of the following questions might be used to stimulate reflection and conversation. Again, use them at your own discretion.

1. Does the awareness grow within you of how much of your life is real gift? That all of your life is a gift?
2. What are some of your feelings about the gifts you have received? Have you taken time to list some of the most significant people as gifts in your life? Some of the forgotten talents?
3. What are some of the "wonders" of your life today?
4. Do you ever feel the closeness of God, that God loves you in a unique way? Do you have a favorite scripture text?

Note: It might be wise at this early stage to talk together about the *ways of praying*—the place, time, posture, all helps used to pray more effectively—so as to determine if retreatants are disposing themselves for listening to God and responding in the best way possible. Are there some *resistances* that need to be talked over?

THIRD DAY
Community Worship
The Day's Theme for Contemplation
The Graced Ones Who Become Dis-graced.
- Prepare the retreatants in these days of the retreat to experience their own *unworthiness* in face of all the love, giftedness, and blessings that God has showered on them as individuals. This experience of unworthiness will often bring with it a deepening awareness of personal refusal to accept love from God or from others. Retreatants will remember certain *sins of commission* and of *omission*, a rejection of gospel values and a turning away from the life of the Spirit.

Texts for Pondering: Luke 15:11-32; Romans 7:14-24; 1 John 1:8-2:11; Luke 6:24-38; Ephesians 2:1-10; Romans 1:18-32; 5:6-21; James 3:2-4:17; Ezekiel 16:1-22; Psalm 51; 2 Peter 2:1-22.

The Grace which we Seek throughout the Day
Retreatants will seek to gain a real sense of what it means to be ungrateful and insensitive to moments of grace. They will seek grace to see the effects of sinful attitudes and actions in their Christian lives and grace to amend in an act of sincere contrition and sorrow.

Individual Sessions
To allow the retreatant to be led more deeply by the Spirit to appreciate the real sense of personal sinfulness in face of the loving, provident care of God, some of the following questions may be helpful. Use them with discretion.
1. What do you think of biblical "sin"? Do you see it as rejection of love in some way?
2. Do you think of sin as being a social evil as well as a personal one? What is your personal definition of sinful attitudes and actions?
3. Describe what sin feels like for you. Do some of these words and concepts come to mind—isolation, separation, alienation, division, lack of sensitivity, estrangement from people, life, self, God?
4. Where does sinfulness reside in your life? In your attitudes? In your head or heart? Do you adjust to sin in yourself and in others? Do you refuse to admit the feelings that sin arouses inside you?
5. Have you honestly, deep-down accepted yourself as a sinner before God? Why not?
6. What is the blindness of personal/social sin? Is there a basic "unspiritual self" in you?
7. How does God's love fit into this dark picture of human sinfulness, whether that sinfulness be individual, social, cultural, or structural? Is my "shadow self" an escape from the loving God?

FOURTH DAY
Community Worship
The Day's Theme for Contemplation
The Forgiver and the Forgiven
- Encourage the retreatant to look at the reality of Christian life: that God has accepted our frailty and failure, our lack of love and selfish weakness. God has accepted us just as we are and loves us, forgives sin in us, and calls us to do the same towards others.

Note: It is not uncommon for a retreatant to show some resistance in accepting personal sinfulness; that is, the full reality of both social sin and individual sin, of what it is and what it has done to the world in which he or she lives.

The opposite tendency may show itself: that he or she will somehow set straight that unworthiness before the Lord, forgetting that it is a sheer grace to recognize one's sinfulness and a sheer grace to seek forgiveness and healing from God.

In other words, be prepared for the retreatant not to believe in God's overwhelming mercy and forgiveness—or at least to be unaware of what it *feels like* to be forgiven so much! There will often be the movement in the retreatant to insist on his or her own meriting of God's forgiveness, of becoming in some manner worthy and deserving of God's love and forgiveness.

It is the failure to understand the overwhelming mystery of God's incomprehensible, undeserved love given to us freely in and through Jesus that blocks persons on retreat from discovering their true relationship with the Savior. This is the blindness of sin—that we will not admit our powerlessness, our inability to save ourselves, the need of the saving availability of Jesus' love.

Texts for Pondering: Isaiah 6:9-10; Philippians 2:1-5; Ephesians 2:4-10, 19-22; Hosea 2:18-25; Psalms 32; 103; 106; 130; Luke 15; 2 Corinthians 5:18-21; Luke 7:36-50; John 9:1-41.

The Grace which we Seek throughout the Day
We seek to experience God's merciful and forgiving love in Jesus, for the grace to know with a deep-felt knowledge that God loves us just as we are and heals us of all our wounds and hurts—if only we let that love penetrate our hearts!

Individual Sessions
As helps to this kind of saving, healing prayer experience, the director might suggest a deep pondering of Romans 8:31-39. Before an image of the crucified Lord, the retreatant might talk with Jesus about the meaning of selfless love and the utter sacrifice that was his and pray for the world in sin and for people who we know are committed to acts of sin, violence, war, and human destruction.

FIFTH DAY
Community Worship
The Day's Theme for Contemplation
The Friend and the Loved Companion:
• Once the praying person accepts the truth that we cannot save ourselves, yet experiences a desperate need to be saved, a new awareness of the meaning of Jesus Christ is experienced deep within the inner soul. Jesus is our unique, personal savior. God has not only accepted us and forgiven and healed us in the love of Jesus; God now calls, invites, and graces the retreatant to intimate relationship; it is a call to be both a *mystic* (with inner commitment) and a prophet (with outer commitment), to preach, teach, and proclaim the gospel values of Jesus Christ in the world of today!

Note: Be prepared for retreatants to experience a real growth in their interior freedom as the retreat moves through the days of sinfulness and the graces prayed for at that time. Look for a clarity of vision coming into the person's own life and a movement to a deeper level of awareness, affecting the individual's total life and all of its relationships. Look for greater calm and stillness in the dialogue sessions, lengthened times of prayer, less to talk about in the formal sessions of meeting.

Once the retreatant has accepted *in depth,* within the *heart's* profoundest places, that he or she has been the object of God's unremitting love from the first moment of life and that that love has been the unbroken bonding all along the way, new horizons begin to open up to the individual in the faith-contact of life.

Texts for Pondering: Genesis 12:1-3; 17:1-8; Exodus 2; 1 Samuel 3:1-14; John 20:7-18; Jeremiah 1; Luke 1:26-38, 46-55; 1 Cor. 1:18-31; John 1:29-51, Mark 3:13-19.

The Grace which we Seek throughout the Day
For a deep-felt knowledge of what it means to be saved by Jesus Christ and to be called by him to share his saving love and ministry in the world today.

Individual Sessions

As the retreat draws to a close, be prepared for the retreatant to begin to wonder about the past and the future, to wonder, in the light of all that has been revealed, about the new awareness of personal relationship to God and about God's love, acceptance, and forgiveness. The retreatant will probably wonder about how he or she can remain free to continue loving and serving God from the heart.

Help the retreatant to meditate on the passage from Luke 24:13-53, the Emmaus encounter where we are assured that the Risen Lord will continue to meet us along the way and challenge us to live more securely in trust, to ponder the word of God, and to meet God at the Lord's Table and in the Christian gathering of fellow believers!

Closing Community Worship

Close the retreat by bringing the entire retreat community together for a time of sharing and celebration around the Eucharist or the Love Feast.

5.

The Preached Retreat

Everyone familiar with making a retreat knows the general setup of a preached retreat, yet somehow it defies description because there are so many different ways a leader of such a retreat can preach it. Fundamentally, its two essential ingredients seem to be 1) a grounding in and a presentation of the Word of God for personal reflection and prayer; and 2) the preaching, the conference, and talks that are given to the retreat group. The retreatants are expected to be *attentive listeners* with some times assigned for quiet, but most of the schedule is filled with formal or informal activities, allowing little or no time for personal direction from the retreat director.

At its best a preached retreat can be a genuinely graced time for all concerned in which the preacher/leader gives the Word of God and the retreatants receive it. Faith is nourished and shared; the Christian community celebrates the power of the Holy Spirit in its midst; and the individual is expected to keep all those words and ponder them deeply (Luke 2:19). The inherent value of this kind of retreat is that it can unleash for the community the internal dynamic of God's Word as proclaimed in Isaiah 55:10-11 (NASB):

As the rain and snow came down from heaven,
And do not return there without watering the earth,
And making it bear and sprout,
And furnishing seed to the sower and bread to the eater;
So shall My word be which goes forth from My mouth; It shall not return to Me empty,
Without accomplishing what I desire, And without succeeding in the matter for which I sent it.

At its worst, a preached retreat could consist of a large number of uninspiring conferences without any personal content, conferences highly academic in nature and unrelated to the everyday affairs of retreatants. The preacher could get caught up in preaching a set of sermons that are truly powerful matter for thought but are not productive of prayerful reflection and affective faith development.

THE POWER OF THE WORD

For the Israelites the word that was verbalized, spoken out, and proclaimed was *a distinct reality* charged with inner power and individual vitality. They conceived God's Word to be *dynamic, dianoetic* and *dialogic*. Here we will say a few words about each of these facets of the biblical word and see how they might apply to our understanding and practice of the preached retreat.

The Word Is Dynamic

- The Word has power because it emerges from a source of divine life and is filled with the vitality and energy of God's own communication of love, life, compassion, and challenge. In releasing the Word, God extends, proclaims, and makes present in created ways the uncreated Self.
- True to its source, the Word accomplishes the very thing it proclaims; it carries out God's purposes without hindrance or impotence.

The Word is Dianoetic

- In accomplishing what it signifies, the Word that is proclaimed also posits the *reality of the speaker;* it reveals the Word person. No one can speak without telling the listener something about the speaker, without revealing the real person behind the words enunciated.
- In putting forth words, a speaker reveals his/her mind and heart; so with God, we can come to know something of the Divine heart by being attentive to God's words.

The Word is Dialogic

- In speaking forth words through the biblical accounts of the Old and New Testaments, God seeks *a response* from those addressed. God wants to engage us in a conversation, a heart-to-heart, a dialogue that leads to a "knowing of each other" that is deep, intimate, and lasting. God's words draw from us a cry of wonder, awe, praise, love, gratitude, sorrow, mercy, need, and emptiness. God's words teach us to *pray.*

THE PREACHED RETREAT ITSELF

When the leader of a preached retreat proclaims for the retreatants the wonderful works of God's love as unfolded in the biblical story, he or she prepares the inner ground for the workings of the Holy Spirit. The leader incarnates the perennial Word for the people of God today.

A certain unity and simplicity can be created in any preached retreat if the talks and conferences are built around the *person* of Jesus Christ. To talk abstractly about the spiritual life, about the basic qualities of living a faith-oriented vocation today may be good on some occasions; but no abstraction will really move a human heart and is even less likely to give strength to its journey to God. The closer the talks come to being shared "insights," personalized views of the gospel story, the better the retreat will be.

To some extent a successful retreat director learns to hide his or her own points of view and interpretations, while at the same time making presentations that are both personable and concrete. Deep theology is excellent, but a retreat should not be exclusively a classroom teaching session. Most people who come to retreats are desperately hungry for God's word and God's illuminating grace and are hardly interested in anything else. They are also immensely grateful if they get the food they are longing for.

PRACTICAL HELPS

The retreat conferences (preaching sessions) should be well prepared and not too long. It is hard to indicate the average length of time because each group is so diverse and the needs are so varied. But if any mistake is to be made, let it be on the side of brevity. Trust the inherent power of God's Word to make up for the lack of human homilizing.

Too many presentations by the leader can fill the minds and hearts of the retreatants with too many stimulating ideas, and there can be little time left for the gentle work of the Holy Spirit. The words of the retreat director should clear the ground and prepare the soil for the implanting of God's seeded word, love, and grace. If there is a plethora of considerations, a whole array of powerful things to reflect upon, and many resolutions to be made, such overabundance can invade the human heart and paralyze it. Too much of the human can impede the working of grace. Retreatants can grow tired and tense and have too much "to do" during certain preached retreats. Such a disposition is unlikely to help in personal prayer and discernment. In fact, one of the indications that the retreat has been a good one is that persons come out from the retreat time refreshed and recreated in their faith life.

The holistic nature of the Word should be carefully kept. The different talks should be interrelated, not disparate topics; one conference should build upon the other. It is not helpful if the retreat group is subjected to three or four different leaders, each with a different stream of thought to present. Ordinarily, retreatants appreciate the simplicity of a one-person approach, even though different facets of the retreat program are in the hands of a variety of helpers.

Peace and restfulness should, of course, be built into every kind of spiritual retreat. It is all the more necessary in the "busy" form of the preached retreat. Since we are to deepen our belief in the power of God's Word in us, we should get rid of the unfortunate iea that the greater the effort we make the more effective the retreat will be. Too much exertion may be just as much an impediment to grace as too little effort. What is important is that the person on retreat be given the time and opportunities to "dialogue with the Lord"; the grace to listen to the inspirations of the Holy Spirit; and the encouragement to carry them out in prayer response. Some time in the retreat schedule should be set for private times of reflection and some time for public worship together as a believing community.

Some concessions to the individual's needs and capacities may be helpful. If there are to be three or four preaching sessions a day, a general rule might be announced early that all *may* attend every conference, but no one *is bound* to attend more than two, for example. This freedom would give more time for an individual's private prayer or space to walk about quietly reflecting and enjoying the contemplative scenery of the retreat setting. At the same time it would not hinder others who feel that they need to listen to more of the retreat conference.

It might also be freeing for individuals if the retreat director were to say early in the retreat that the materials presented in the preaching sessions are only "suggestions" for personal reflection. Admittedly, for many to follow the talks in their personal prayer may be the best way to meet God; but for some, following the preacher's ideas too closely may lead to frustration and render the person too structured to enjoy the peaceful work of the Holy Spirit. The spiritual life and inner growth have their own dynamic laws, and no one can tamper with them without paying some penalty. So if the talks do not help a person, that individual should be allowed to get the food that he/she needs in another way. Often, times of wordless quiet, where one remains in peaceful, waiting attentiveness, are the times of real grace.

Finally, there needs to be some mention of the group discussions and sharing sessions that make up so many of the "preached retreat" settings. If the small groups that meet share the insights received and affirm the role of how God works in their lives, then the meetings can have great formative value. Personal encounter with God's dynamic, dianoetic, and dialogic word always leads toward creating Christian community—"For wherever two or three are gathered in my name . . ." (Matt. 18:20). Once a Christian has learned to some degree to live in the Spirit, then the greatest gift he or she can give is to enrich others with the shared gift of that religious experience. The church has suffered much harm from an extreme individualism; we need to realize our oneness in Christ and give practical expression to this unity. A preached retreat can continue to offer the Christian community a time and a place for deep, personal growth—a time of listening to God's word in the scriptures in the preacher's exposition, in shared human dialogue.

> If you make my Word your home,
> you will be my disciples,
> You will learn the truth
> and the truth will set you free.
> —John 8:31-32, paraphrase

A PREACHED RETREAT DESIGN

Group Size: adaptable to circumstances of time and place

Length of Retreat: 1 to 3 days

The Retreat Structure

The following distribution of time tries to strike a reasonable balance between some time for personal freedom and prayer as well as time for group listening and sharing, between the need to attend conferences and the need to be in undisturbed quiet reflection.

This format has been used often and has proved successful with a wide variety of retreat groups. The times are obviously hypothetical and can be varied according to local needs. It is assumed that there will be at least two talks a day; the third conference time is adaptable to the practical situation encountered.

Order of the Day

6:30 A.M. —Wake-up Call

7:00 A.M. —Individual Quiet Time / Reflection on matter presented the previous evening

8:00 A.M. —Breakfast

9:00 A.M. —Conference 1 (about 30 minutes)

9:30 A.M. —Break / Time for Personal Prayer, Quiet Reflection, Journal Writing

10:30 A.M. —Small Group Sharing

11:30 A.M. —Break / Time for Moving About

12:00 Noon—Lunch

1:00 P.M. —A time of Solitude, Rest / Reading, Reflection, and Prayer

3:00 P.M. —Conference 2 (about 45 minutes)

3:45 P.M. —Break

4:00 P.M. —Time Apart / Reflection and Prayer, Reading and Personal Solitude

4:30 P.M. —Small Group Sharing

5:30 P.M. —Dinner

7:00 P.M. —Recreation, Reflection, Rest

8:00 P.M. —Conference 3 (about one hour). Group Sharing and/or Discussion of the Day's Presentations

9:00 P.M. —Worship / Agape / Singing / Communion

9:30 P.M. —Solitude and Rest

It is essential that even this program should not be perceived rigidly; both the searcher/director and the retreatants should make adaptations according to the rhythms of the retreat and the local needs. More space could be created for large group sharing/discussions or time could be allowed for individuals to see the retreat leader alone for private consultations.

The last day could end with a worship service either just before lunch and departure or after the group sharing session in the late afternoon.

FIRST DAY

The opening session may begin at 10:30 A.M. If so, you would begin following the "order of the day" after lunch, rearranging the schedule as is necessary to provide time for three "conference" periods.

Setting the Scene (about 30 minutes)
1. *Words of Welcome:* housekeeping details / explaining the order of the day and possible adaptations
2. *Opening Talk*
   The opening talk might consist of the following components:
   • Scripture Reading: John 1:35-39 (RSV)

   The next day again John was standing with two of his disciples; and he looked at Jesus as he walked, and said, "Behold, the Lamb of God!" The two disciples heard him say this, and they followed Jesus. Jesus turned, and saw them following, and said to them, "What do you seek?" And they said to him, "Rabbi (which means Teacher), where are you staying?" He said to them, "Come and see." They came and saw where he was staying; and they stayed with him that day.

   • Purpose of the Retreat
   Staying with God, listening to God's words, imbibing God's power, and resting in the presence of God's love.
   Asking the grace during the days:
      To know more intimately
      To love more ardently,
      To follow more closely.
   • The Word of God as Power in Our Lives (Isa. 55:10-11; Deut. 30:11-14)
   A Dynamic Word.   It has power because it emerges from the very mouth of the all-loving, all-powerful and ever-faithful God. It is a presence of Yahweh to the chosen people that gives life, promotes life, and challenges life to grow more fruitfully (Deut. 30:15-20).

   A Dianoetic Word.   It invites us to know, to "see," to experience God. It tells us what is on God's mind. It shares what is in God's heart, and it makes available to the listener in faith the very character of the "mysterious other" as caring, concerned Parent.

   A Dialogic Word.   It expects that the human heart, touched by the divine spark, will respond to the message of life and hope, assurance and guidance promised. It elicits a prayer from the core of all created beings; it helps us to cry aloud our human joys and pains, our consolations and confusions, our times of darkness and our need for light.
3. *Ten-Minute, Stand-up Break*

Conference 1

1. *Scripture Reading:* John 1:1-18 (RSV)

   In the beginning was the Word,
      and the Word was with God,
      And the Word was God.
   He was in the beginning with God;
   All things were made through him,
      and without him was not anything
      made that was made.

In him was life,
    and the life was the light
    of men.
The Light shines in the darkness,
    and the darkness had not overcome it.

2. *The Preached Word*
The Abiding Beauty of Hymns, Canticles, and Songs

This introduction to John's Gospel is a beautiful piece of poetry and a well-honed Christian hymn. It has had a special place in the hearts of Christians from the very beginning of their faith life. It may be the most beautiful passage, the best-loved song in all of Christian literature.

Our prayerful reflection can never exhaust the depths of these few verses; they lead us to a real insight into the tremendous mystery of the Incarnatio.

• The Old Testament Songs. The Book of Psalms, 150 hymns of God's people, expresses very vividly the *dialogic* nature of Christian prayer—our human response to God's initiatives in our lives. These hymns include songs of love, praise, awe and wonder in the presence of such a caring, providing God (Pss. 19; 23; 51; 89; 98). They also include canticles of thanksgiving, gratitude, joy for God's kindness, for God's generosity and caring concern for the lowly (Pss. 84-86; 92).

• The New Testament Hymns. The writings of Paul are filled with the most lovely songs of the early Christian communities. They articulate the depths of our need to respond to the Lord's gifts and include hymns that celebrate the giftedness of our baptismal life, the glory of being alive in Jesus, the joy of being a follower of the "way" (1 Cor. 13:1-12, hymn of love; Phil. 2:6-11, hymn celebrating Jesus as Servant; Eph. 1:1-14, hymn celebrating God's plan for us; Gospel hymns include Luke 1:36-55, Mary's Magnificat, and John 15:1-11, hymn of Jesus' love).

The Prologue of John's Gospel: These verses compose a hymn that includes main themes for prayer. They include God's abiding presence; God's constant desires to companion us; Jesus' life as light for our human darkness, as life for all forms of our deadness, as hope for all of our loneliness and fears; and power given to God's believing people, to be incarnated into the family of God, to share the mystery as brothers and sisters of Jesus in the divine family embrace.

• The Personal Poetry, Song, Music of Our Own Lives: What "song" do we sing: a poem of praise and joy? A song of sadness and fear? A dirge for all the past? An alleluia or a lament? A *magnificat* or the "blues"?

Take time to ponder the giftedness of our lives: the "wonders" of our 1980s existence—the fidelity of God as companion to us in and through the risen life of Jesus and the Holy Spirit, who dwells within us (John 14:15-17)!

Conference 2

1. *Scripture Reading:* John 1:6-8, 15, 19-34 (RSV)

There was a man sent from God, whose name was John.
    He came for testimony, to bear witness to the light,
    that all might believe
    through him.
He was not the light,
    but came to bear witness to the light.
John . . . cried, "This was he of whom I said:
    "He who comes after me
    ranks before me,
    for he was before me."

2. *The Preached Word*
The Herald of Jesus Christ.   John the Baptizer was a voice that cried in the wilderness and made straight the way for the coming of the Lord.

- **John's Testimony.** John points out Jesus as the "Lamb of God," the symbol of the suffering savior, the *servant* as proclaimed in Isaiah 52:13-53:12. He testifies to the *fact* that Jesus is the "Son of God," the chosen one of the race. John lets us know what kind of a messiah we are dealing with, totally human (pain) and totally divine (glory). We cannot have one without the other when we accept the total reality of Jesus!
- **Christian Witness.** Our witness is not so much what we do for the Lord, but what we have been "called," "chosen" to do for God's kingdom. We come to realize that *we are special*, as was John, that we are called to show forth the power that has been given us, to realize that whatever our "desert" may be God continues to speak the Word there, telling us how important we are to the spreading of the Word and our Creator's kingdom.

From the very start, Psalm 8 reminds us of our *human dignity* and the dignity of all human beings. Ponder the meanings of these texts: Psalm 139; Isaiah 43:1-5; John 14:1-31; Matthew 6:25-34; Romans 8:28-39; Ephesians 3:14-21.

- **The Call to Intimacy with the Lord.** We are called to come and see (John 1:35-51). How are we attracted to God in our lives? How do we attract others into God's company?

Conference 3

This could be a brief preparation for the morning (7:00-8:00) period of reflective quiet and prayer before breakfast, a time to pull together some of the sharings of the small groups, with some clarifications and deepenings of the matter presented and experienced by the retreatants.

1. *Scripture Reading:* John 2:1-12—The Signs of Jesus

For John, a *sign* was a special *happening* (miracle) which symbolizes a spiritual truth about Jesus and reveals to us something of who he is and draws us to faith in his person. There are seven such signs in this Gospel; some of them we will use for prayer during this retreat:

Turning water into wine (2:1-11)
Curing the official's son (4:46-54)
Healing the lame man at the pool (5:2-9)
Feeding the five thousand (6:4-13)
Walking on water (6:16-21)
Curing the man born blind (9:1-41)
The raising of Lazarus (11:1-44)

2. *The Preached Word*

The Miracle of Cana—the First of Jesus' Signs
- Meal as the context / the importance of meal scenes in the Gospels / the kingdom comes to the hungry (cf. Isa. 54:4-8; Hos. 1-3; Matt. 22:1-14; Luke 24:28-43)
- The banquet theology of the Bible
    union and communion; celebration of life, friendship, weddings, funerals
    truth revealed over a meal; haves and have-nots
    healing and forgiveness when bread is broken and shared; a meal in common is a time for making peace and reconciling opposites
- Food as a universal language
    national foods, cultural intimacy, gracious hospitality centers on food and drink
    poverty or an abundance; healthy or sick; hopeless or supremely satisfied—all are one at the table, the natural *instinct* to share food with others!
- The Source of Christian nourishment
    table fellowship with the Risen Lord and with one another / the value of the Lord's Supper / the value of meals shared in faith and hope. God's Word deeply imbibed sets up a hunger for the bread of life (cf. Luke 24:13ff).
- Some favorite New Testament meal scenes: Mark 6:30-44; Luke 19:1-10; 24:13-49; John 6:1-14.

3. *Materials for Personal Reflection Tomorrow Morning* (7:00-8:00 A.M.)

This communicating God speaks to us in so many different ways, from a whole world of varied resources, and in all kinds of life experiences:

• Nature and Creation Words: Psalm 8; 104; Job 38-39.
• The Saving Word in Our Own Lives: Psalm 23; 139; Isaiah 43; Matthew 6:25-34; John 15:1-27
• The Jesus Word: his life, ministry, his saving death, his glorious resurrection, his abiding Spirit among us and within us, his call to preach the Good News to the whole world: Matt. 28:11-20.

SECOND DAY
Conference 1

1. *Scripture Reading:* John 2:1-12—The Woman and Mother

When the wine gave out, the mother of Jesus said to him: "They have no wine." And Jesus said to her: "O woman, what have you to do with me? My hour has not yet come." His mother said to the servants: "Do whatever he tells you."   (RSV)

2. *The Preached Word*

The Role of the Woman-Mother

• Mary is seen here as a dynamic, sensitive, energizing character; she sees the need of the human situation and responds to the inner movements of her caring heart for the young couple. Mary serves as a corrective to Jesus' concern about the appropriate time for his public ministry to begin; his hour becomes NOW!

• The *woman* as symbol of the Christian life:

Trust: Mary, the Christian model, can draw from Jesus the power of his messianic personhood. She does what the woman in Mark 7:24-30 will later do—draw healing power from the depths of Jesus' person. It helps us to realize the power we can have from Jesus if we trust in the prayer of petition and supplication.

Hospitality: Mary has the necessary zest for human living. She has a nurturing heart open to the plight of others, and she knows what it means to love her son freely so that real change can occur. She demonstrates the difference that one motivated Christian heart can really make in any needy situation!

Total giving: This woman can be at the first celebration as well as at the last. She can sit here and enjoy and also stand at the cross and grieve over the mystery of being a follower of Jesus (John 19:25ff).

Hope-filled: Out of this ending in Jesus' final "hour" is born the small remnant of Jesus' followers who gather in an upper room. Present at the core of that community, the woman waits with the rest of the disciples for promises to be fulfilled, for the future to emerge, for the breaking in of the new age, for the new wine for all the people of God to drink without regret.

Conference 2

1. *Scripture Reading:* John 4:46-54—The Healed Son

The official said to him, "Sir, come before my child dies." Jesus said to him, "Go, your son will live." The man believed the word that Jesus spoke to him and went his way. As he was going down, his servants met him and told him that his son was living. (RSV)

The Preached Word

• Faith in Jesus: This second sign that Jesus performed has a twofold impact: it stresses *trust* in Jesus' person and power and thus is a culmination of the scenes that come before this one in John's Gospel. It also stresses Jesus' *desire to give life,* and this introduces one of the major themes of the Fourth Gospel.

- Progress in Faith: A glance at the individuals that have come before us in the pages of this Gospel tells us that there is a gradual *progression* in the quality of the faith expressed by these people towards Jesus. Look at these three, for example:

   Nicodemus (3:1-15): The Jewish Pharisee listens openly to Jesus in the dark of his night and comes to acknowledge Jesus as Rabbi, or learned Teacher. At this first encounter, however, we do not get a very clear commitment to Jesus or a very strong idea of his wanting to be a disciple.

   Samaritan woman (4:1-30): This half-pagan, half-Jewish individual recognizes that Jesus is some kind of special prophet, that he might even be the long-expected Messiah. She does lead her townfolk to Jesus, and these come to have faith in Jesus.

   Roman official (4:46-54): The Gentile foreigner stands before Jesus asking for a "sign." He makes a pure act of trust and a clear sign is given of his own faith in the power of Jesus' word. He goes away knowing that his son will be cured although at the moment he has no positive human proof.

- Growth in Christian Faith Life: "Lord, we believe, help our unbelief!" Obstacles to growth in our belief are:
   - our fears, our lack of trust in the personal provident care of the Risen Jesus,
   - some of our hidden, unresolved angers, our unhealed hurts, our painful memories of past injustice,
   - our poor self-image, our lack of self-confidence, our family problems, discouragements, and lack of support.

Conference 3

1. *Scripture Reading:* John 5:2-18—The Third Sign
2. *The Preached Word*

   Note: Again, this presentation could be a brief outline of some matter for the morning prayer time (7:00-8:00 A.M.) before breakfast, a time to pull together some of the group's sharings on the experience, questions, and discussions of the day.

   - For John, the third special happening, the miracle story of the cure of the lame man, is a good opportunity to expose for the reader the clear conditions under which the healing power of Jesus operated. Jesus began by asking the man if he *wanted* to be cured; it is possible that some people really don't want to be healed. They prefer being "in pain," getting the attention of others. Some people seem to enjoy self-pitying behavior and must keep up levels of dependence on others that give them some inner, confused sense of "being important."

      We need to ask ourselves about our own desires to meet the Lord, to ask for the deep healing that we need in our own relationships. The first essential for receiving the power of his mending word is the *deep desire* for it. Jesus asks, "What can I do for you?" So we must ask ourselves, "Is our passion to live life at its fullest, to turn over to Jesus the deepest hurts, the long-standing rejections, the pain of our hurts, the unforgiving heart, the creeping carelessness, and the inability to reach out to those who offend us?"

      Jesus' command to the lame person to attempt the impossible—"Get up!"—signals the need for self-help, for cooperation with the grace of God. We need to know our *strengths* so that we can let the Lord use all the power that is in us. We must make a human effort to respond to the initiatives of Jesus.

      Jesus works his wonders on those who believe and trust him, but his activity often brings with it a barrage of criticism and complaint from others. Jesus is often seen being attentive to the outcasts of his day—the sick, the poor, the lepers, the marginal people—and the healing caused *stress* in those who did not accept his ways and could not tolerate his openness.

      Does Jesus in our own day cause people stress? How and in what degree? Does he still eat with sinners; does he still touch leprous flesh; does he still lift up the poor, feed the hungry, and tend the sick? How do you see that carried on in your own lives? Where is the *compassion* of Jesus in our own day?

3. *Materials for Personal Reflection Tomorrow Morning* (7:00-8:00 A.M.)

Jesus comes to us with the question, "What do you want me to do for you?"

a. Read Mark 10:46-52; John 5:2-18

b. Reflect upon your responses to the following questions:
   - What do you want Jesus to do for you? What is your deepest desire and secret motivation for all of life?
   - What effort are you making to make yourself available to Jesus so that he may speak his *word* to you?
   - Do you have faith today that Jesus is granting your heart's desire?

c. Write your morning prayer to God in the form of a letter with three paragraphs. Respond to each of the questions above in the three paragraphs.

THIRD DAY

The Closing Conference

1. *Scripture Reading:* John 6:16-21—The Fifth Sign

2. *The Preached Word*

In this miracle story, two important truths about Jesus are proclaimed. First, he is the source of our *trust* in troubled times, a refuge for a stormy and fear-filled human experience. Jesus is clearly seen as sensitive to human need and ready to come to your assistance on his own initiative. Secondly, Jesus, in using the expression "It is I, do not be afraid" (6:20, RSV) at the recognition point in the story, is identifying himself with the God of the Old Testament as Yahweh acted in Exodus 3:14. Yahweh said: "I AM WHO I AM." "Say this to the people of Israel, 'I AM has sent me to you.'" See also Isaiah 41:9: "You are my servant, I have chosen you . . . fear not, for I am with you."

   - The Parables in John's Gospel

     Seven parables in John's Gospel form a series of seven cameos. They tell of Jesus' deep commitment to the human scene, to us as disciples and followers. Each parable is a call to *deeper intimacy* with him:

     —I AM the Bread of Life (6:35)
     —I AM the Light of the World (8:12)
     —I AM the Door of the Sheepfold (10:7)
     —I AM the Good Shepherd (10:11)
     —I AM the Resurrection and the Life (11:25)
     —I AM the Way, and the Truth, and the Life (14:6)
     —I AM the True Vine (15:1)

   - The Bread of Life (6:1-15, 22-51*a*, 51*b*-58, 60-71)—The Fourth Sign

     The central event of this famous sixth chapter is the multiplication of the loaves and fish, a scene rich with overtones of the eucharistic supper (Mark 6:37-44). There are two major themes that color this sign:

     The *Sapiential:* The bread of life is God's revealing word; to eat this bread is to accept deeply the person and message of Jesus. It means saying a total YES to Jesus.

     The *Sacramental:* The bread is Jesus' total self; eternal life comes from communion in the Lord's flesh and blood. The importance of the Lord's Supper is that it is where we confront his real presence as food for the Christian journey.

   - Our role as eucharistic people: We are sent forth to feed others with the Word and Sacrament, to provide bread for the world, and to be a justice and peace people!

3. *The Eucharist*

6.

The Private Retreat

Earlier we spoke of retreats as those times set apart in the daily routine to be in conscious communion with God. Retreats may be for a few moments or for several days. Thus, retreat time is available to everyone.

Often, however, the time available for solitude in the midst of a hectic daily schedule is not sufficient for the review and reflection of our lives and the discipline which is essential for sustaining a mature spiritual growth. It is in this respect that private retreats become of importance.

Private retreats are most beneficial when included as a regular part of our spiritual discipline. A twenty-four hour time period is desirable; however, we must adjust the hours to fit the demands of our schedule. Six to eight hours alone each month will accrue tremendous spiritual benefit in our lives.

The setting for the private retreat is very important. Retreatants will gain by going to a place away from everyday trappings—a house of prayer; a comfortable camp; a room in a church; a tent on the prairie; or, if need be, an unused room in the home.

The private retreat should follow a simple schedule of silent listening and meditation, reading scripture and devotional favorites, reviewing our spiritual journey, journal writing, and rest. The day may be spent as follows:

Silent listening. The retreat should begin with at least thirty minutes of silence given to quieting the noises within and without. Allow the body, mind, and spirit to let go of the stresses and weight of the daily grind and enter into the peace of mind Christ offers to all who will go away with him (Mark 6:30-31).

Often spiritual music will help lead one into a mood of receptivity and quietness. Relax in a comfortable chair or lie on the floor, letting the music flow over you.

Meditation and praying the scripture. When the heart and mind are sufficiently quiet, turn your attention to the Word of God in the Gospels, or in some other part of scripture. It is always good to begin with a story about Jesus or some other biblical character in order that you may be drawn into the movement, sounds, and scenes of the Word.

Do not read too many verses at a time. It is better to read only the verses needed to tell one incident in the life of those about whom you are reading. Read the story as though you were eating a leisurely meal, taking time to savor each phrase and verse. Let your reading lead you into meditation, and your meditation into prayer.

A simple method for praying the scripture was taught by St. Benedict, and later by Martin Luther. For learning this simple, but effective method, see footnote 1 for chapter 6.

Readings for reflection and spiritual enjoyment. You may want to take a book along by such authors as Henri Nouwen, Carlo Carretto, Anthony Bloom, Hanna Whitehall Smith, Evelyn Underhill. Or you may prefer an anthology of spiritual readings such as the one we have prepared for our own use. This book, *A Guide to Prayer for Ministers and Other Servants*, also contains twelve private retreat models, as well as prayer resources for every day of the year.

Review and reflection. This is a time to take stock of one's own life before God. Begin by reviewing your journal entries for the past month, or more. Then review the covenants you have made with God, yourself, and others with an eye to seeing how well you have kept them.

Next you may want to consider a set of spiritual accountability questions, writing your responses to each in your journal.[2] You will then have this writing to assist your review during your next private retreat.

Prayerful listening and reflection. Laying all books and pen aside, bring mind and heart together in silence before God. Allow God to speak to you from all you have read, felt, and written. You may want to sit in silence, or enjoy a leisurely walk in a quiet place away from noise and people distractions.

Rest. It is now time to rest mind and heart to allow time for mental digestion of all you have experienced in the retreat. A twenty–minute nap at the right time can greatly facilitate your spiritual listening.

The boundary between our subconscious and conscious self is most permeable during the moments bridging wakefulness and sleep. In these minutes the conscious is able to store information in the pantry of its subconscious, and the subconscious is able to send messages freely to the conscious. During the sleep God is able to communicate more freely to the deeper levels of our subconscious.

If while on retreat you take some time for rest, at the right time, you may find it as important to your spiritual growth as the time spent in other activities.

Exercise. If you are on a twenty-four hour retreat, you will want to take some form of vigorous exercise—swimming, jogging, or walking.

Repeating the process. If your retreat allows you sufficient time, you can simply repeat the process using new scriptures and readings.

If possible we strongly encourage you to receive the Lord's Supper toward the end of the retreat. It is always good to take the Lord's Supper, since it allows the Word to come to us through all five physical senses, as well as through the intuitive sense.

Following are retreat outlines for three private retreats. The first two are taken from our book, *A Guide to Prayer For Ministers and Other Servants*. The third is a retreat based upon a reading of Mark's Gospel. This is a favorite of ours for private retreat during the Lenten season.

PRIVATE RETREAT DESIGN 1

The Sinner's Friend

Schedule

Arrival

Thirty Minutes of Silent Listening

Scripture Readings
    Luke 15:1-10; 7:36-50; John 4:7-42; Romans 5:1-11

Readings for Reflection (Use pp. 394–398 in *A Guide to Prayer* for both cycles of readings for reflection.)

Reflection

Prayer

Journal Writing

Recreation

Rest

Repeat Cycle of Scripture Reading, Readings for Reflection, Reflection, Prayer, and Journal Writing

Thirty Minutes of Silent Reflection

Holy Communion

Benediction

PRIVATE RETREAT DESIGN 2

God Cares for Us

Schedule

Arrival

Thirty Minutes of Silent Listening

Scripture Readings
Luke 12:22-34; Psalm 121; John 14:15-31; 2 Corinthians 1:3-22

Readings for Reflection (Use pp. 370–374 in *A Guide to Prayer* for both cycles of readings for reflection.)

Reflection

Prayer

Journal Writing

Recreation

Rest

Repeat Cycle of Scripture Readings, Readings for Reflection, Reflection, Prayer, and Journal Writing

Thirty Minutes of Silent Reflection

Holy Communion

Benediction

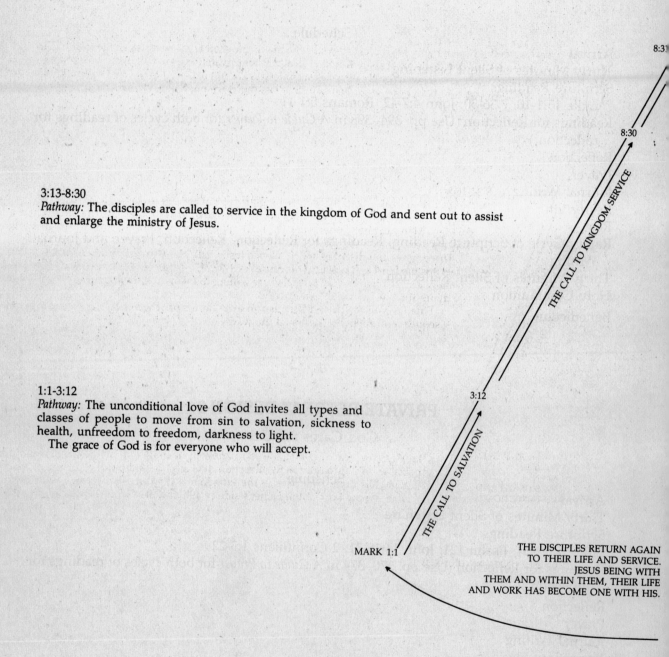

8:31

8:30

3:13-8:30
Pathway: The disciples are called to service in the kingdom of God and sent out to assist and enlarge the ministry of Jesus.

THE CALL TO KINGDOM SERVICE

1:1-3:12
Pathway: The unconditional love of God invites all types and classes of people to move from sin to salvation, sickness to health, unfreedom to freedom, darkness to light.
    The grace of God is for everyone who will accept.

3:12

THE CALL TO SALVATION

MARK 1:1

THE DISCIPLES RETURN AGAIN
TO THEIR LIFE AND SERVICE.
JESUS BEING WITH
THEM AND WITHIN THEM, THEIR LIFE
AND WORK HAS BECOME ONE WITH HIS.

THE CYCLE OF LOVE

CHRISTIAN GROWTH
BY ST. MARK

The great "watershed" passage in Mark; Jesus reveals the messianic secret that he must suffer and die. To be fully human means that Jesus must share humans' death. Peter privately tries to talk him out of his plan to suffer and die (v 32); and Jesus strongly declares such desires are not of God (v 33). From this moment on many disciples begin to turn away from Jesus until at last there are none left. He dies alone.

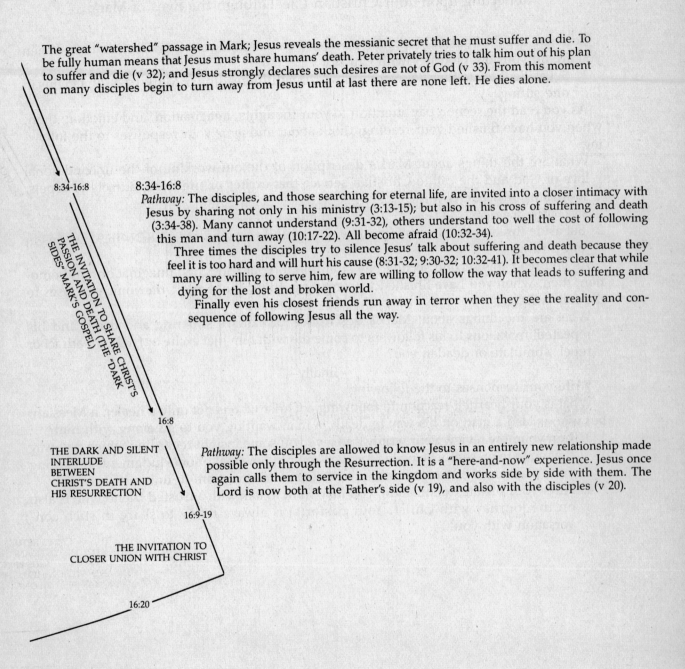

8:34-16:8

8:34-16:8

Pathway: The disciples, and those searching for eternal life, are invited into a closer intimacy with Jesus by sharing not only in his ministry (3:13-15); but also in his cross of suffering and death (3:34-38). Many cannot understand (9:31-32), others understand too well the cost of following this man and turn away (10:17-22). All become afraid (10:32-34).

Three times the disciples try to silence Jesus' talk about suffering and death because they feel it is too hard and will hurt his cause (8:31-32; 9:30-32; 10:32-41). It becomes clear that while many are willing to serve him, few are willing to follow the way that leads to suffering and dying for the lost and broken world.

Finally even his closest friends run away in terror when they see the reality and consequence of following Jesus all the way.

THE INVITATION TO SHARE CHRIST'S PASSION AND DEATH (THE 'DARK SIDES' MARK'S GOSPEL)

16:8

THE DARK AND SILENT
INTERLUDE
BETWEEN
CHRIST'S DEATH AND
HIS RESURRECTION

Pathway: The disciples are allowed to know Jesus in an entirely new relationship made possible only through the Resurrection. It is a "here-and-now" experience. Jesus once again calls them to service in the kingdom and works side by side with them. The Lord is now both at the Father's side (v 19), and also with the disciples (v 20).

16:9-19

THE INVITATION TO
CLOSER UNION WITH CHRIST

16:20

BEGINS AGAIN

PRIVATE RETREAT DESIGN 3

Reflecting upon Your Christian Life Through the Eyes of Mark

You may use the Book of Mark for a private examination of your own Christian life. When you are on your own journey with Christ:

1. Set aside three to four hours for a slow, thoughtful reading of Mark 1:1-8:30. Do this in one sitting.

As you read the section pay attention to your thoughts, imagination, and emotion; then, when you have finished your reading, think about and *write* your responses to the following:

What are the things about Mark's description of the out-working of the unconditional love of God and the call to Christian service that excites or frightens, attracts or repels, stimulates or deadens you?

—then—

2. Set aside three to four hours for a slow, thoughtful reading of Mark 8:31–16:9. Do this in one sitting.

As you read this second section pay attention to your thoughts, imagination, and emotion; then, when you have finished your reading, think about and *write* your responses to the following:

What are the things about Mark's description of Christ's suffering and death and his repeated invitations to his followers to come die with him that excite or frighten, attract or repel, stimulate or deaden you?

—finally—

Write your responses to the following:

What is your heartfelt reaction to following a Christ who is not only a healer, a Messiah, but who is also a man on his way to death, a man wanting you to go along with him?

3. Can you now review your writings to give you some insight regarding which pathway that you are presently being led to take? You can now make some judgments regarding your place on the Way that leads to the life of resurrection, to union with Christ.

4. After your private examination, you may want to talk with a trusted friend who is also on the journey with Christ. Your pastor(s) is always ready to share in such conversation with you.

7.

Conclusion

In preparing this book we have found it difficult to resist the temptation to write more commentary on the process of spiritual growth and on the actual dynamics of retreats. We have felt it best, however, to prepare this manual with one focus—to give you a set of tools to use in conducting a retreat.

There are, however, one or two items of such importance that we have decided to speak to them briefly.

1. Spiritual life retreats are a very small but important element of our spiritual formation. More important is the spirituality of Sunday worship in the church the retreatant attends, belonging to a covenant community of four to twelve persons, and receiving spiritual guidance from a person who is him/herself a deeply spiritual, "connected" person.

2. Few persons today have an awareness of the presence of God. When they do it is only for a brief moment and is often dismissed as illusionary.

A noted Eastern guru was guest at a Benedictine monastery in Spain where I was staying for a month-long private retreat. Before leaving, the guru said to the monks, "I am disappointed in what I found here, for I see you have given up the personal experience of the Christian Gospels for a Rule. Thousands of Westerners today are coming to Eastern yoga. But it does not satisfy their deep longings, because Eastern yoga is for the Eastern mind, which is very different from the Western mind. The people who come to you are searching for the Christian yoga, which they could find in a simple reading and experience of the four Gospels, but your Rule is not that."

I was cut to the heart by his words. Thousands of people today are filing into monastaries, churches, and retreats looking for the Christian yoga which is the very heartbeat of the four Gospels. But often they go away not having seen or experienced Jesus; either in our "rules," our liturgies, or our programs in us!

The best gift you have to offer your retreatants is that you simply *be* an evangel of the gospel. What you share of your own journey, your witness to your own faith-full search and discovery, is far more important than the retreat process you follow.

If you aren't on a journey with Christ, if you do not have an awareness of the presence of God in your life as a living reality, if you are not in search and discovery of the simple message of the Gospels, then the retreat will likely be a disappointing experience for you and the retreatants.

But if you are giving yourself to the message of the Gospels, you will be **a gift to the** retreatant. Then, if you prepare your design well, the retreat will be a lifegiving experience for you and for all who come to be with you.

One other thing in respect to the comments of the guru—there is a marvelous power in the Story and the stories in the four Gospels. For one thing, so many of them are incomplete! Have you ever wondered whether the elder son finally went into the celebration with his father in the story of "the prodigal father" (Luke 15:11-32)? Or have you ever wondered what the accountants found when they audited Zacchaeus's books to ascertain whether he had defrauded anyone in their tax payments (Luke 19:1-10)?

Jesus and the Gospel writers deliberately left the stories incomplete because these are not merely the stories of an elder son, or Zacchaeus. These are stories about us—and we alone can decide the ending. For this reason the Gospels are your most powerful source of material for retreats. You can tell one story, and it will be intensely personal for every retreatant as you enable (through your design) each one to finish the story in their own experience.

Speaking of the retreatants' own experience points to an important guideline. Don't let persons argue or try to change another's view, or reaction to, the Scriptures. And don't give them your "educated wisdom" either. Since Jesus left the stories incomplete, you can do likewise. A retreat is not a crash course in hermeneutics. It's an invitation for each person to write the fifth gospel—the Good News according to their own lives. Trust the spirit of Jesus to not lead them astray in their own handling of the stories.

There is one other resource which probably stands on par with the Gospels; that is the Book of Psalms. At least 95 percent of the persons who come to your retreats will be experiencing difficulty with prayer. The psalms are prayers written under inspiration of the Holy Spirit. They are for *all* people at *all* times. Perhaps the greatest favor we can do for persons who want to pray is to relieve them of the guilt and frustration of trying to fashion their own prayer words.

Since the Spirit gave us the psalms we can feel good about praying them, and we can know that the Spirit wants to pray them through us (Rom. 8:26-27). There is at least one psalm-prayer for every condition experienced by any person.

Finally, if you do these three things in any retreat it will be a success:

1. Give simple, transparent witness to your own love for and life with Jesus Christ.
2. Allow retreatants to reflect upon and tell the stories of their own journeys toward and/ or away from Christ.
3. Teach people how to use the psalms as a never-ending source of prayers.

Please let us hear from you. We want to know if our designs are helpful, and we want you to share your designs with us.

Notes

Preface

1. Rueben P. Job and Norman Shawchuck, *A Guide to Prayer for Ministers and Other Servants* (Nashville: The Upper Room, 1983). Introduces twelve day-long retreat models for your private retreat each month.

Chapter 1   Wandering toward the Promised Land

1. Dietrich Bonhoeffer, *Life Together* (New York: Harper & Brothers, 1954), p. 23.
2. For in-depth treatment of this important truth see Henri Nouwen, *Reaching Out* (Garden City, N.Y.: Doubleday, 1975).

Chapter 2   The Pathways to Growth in the Spiritual Life

1. See Evelyn Underhill, "The Spiritual Exercises of Christ" in *The Light of Christ* (London: Logmans, Green & Co, Ltd., 1944).

Introduction to Part 2

1. The Emmaus walk is a highly structured dialogical retreat. For information, contact The Upper Room, P.O. Box 189, Nashville, TN 37202.

Chapter 3   The Dialogical Retreat

1. Cassette tapes of music are available to facilitate meditation and prayer. Two companies whose cassettes we use are North American Liturgy Resources, Phoenix, Arizona; and the St. Louis Jesuits, St. Louis, Missouri.
2. A resource for the group's daily discipline is the aforementioned *A Guide to Prayer for Ministers and Other Servants* by Job and Shawchuck (Nashville: The Upper Room, 1983).

Chapter 4   The Personally Guided Retreat

1. Maxie Dunnam, *Alive in Christ* (Nashville: Abingdon, 1982), p. 9.
2. An excellent resource for daily discipline and for retreats is Job and Shawchuck, *A Guide to Prayer for Ministers and Other Servants* (Nashville: The Upper Room, 1983).

Chapter 6   The Private Retreat

1. The Benedictine Method can be found in Sadhana, *A Way to God*, Exercise 33, pp. 101-105.
2. For example, the questions used by the early band of John Wesley, see Appendix E, *The Early Methodist Class Meeting* (Nashville: Discipleship Resources, 1985).

Annotated Bibliography

Below is a list of resources we consider "must" reading for persons conducting spiritual life retreats.

1. Adams, Lane. *How Come It's Taking Me So Long to Get Better?* Wheaton, Ill: Tyndale, 1975.

   Helpful responses to some of the most often asked questions in a retreat.

2. Evely, Louis. *We Dare to Say Our Father.* New York: Doubleday, 1975.

   Excellent resource for a guided or preached retreat on the subject of the Lord's Prayer.

3. Fleming, David J. *The Spiritual Exercises: A Literal Translation and a Contemporary Reading.* St. Louis: The Institute of Jesuit Sources, 1978.

   Modern reading of the spiritual exercises of St. Ignatius for guided retreats and spiritual direction.

4. Foster, Richard. *Celebration of Discipline.* San Francisco: Harper & Row, 1978.

   The best discussion of the spiritual disciplines in a single text.

5. Holmes, Urban T. *Spirituality For Ministry.* San Francisco: Harper & Row, 1982.

   Important reading for anyone conducting retreats for persons engaged in professional ministry.

6. Job, Rueben P. and Shawchuck, Norman. *A Guide to Prayer for Ministers and Other Servants.* Nashville: The Upper Room, 1983.

   Prepared out of the authors' own experience in daily discipline and retreats. This resource is one of the most profitable resources for retreat leaders.

7. Nouwen, Henri. *The Living Reminder.* New York: The Seabury Press, 1981.

   Excellent discussion of the interrelationship of ministry and spirituality. We recommend all of Nouwen's books for your reading.

APPENDIX I

Spiritual Guidance, Intercessory Prayer, Pastoral Counseling, Counseling Therapy

A CHART OF SIMILARITIES AND DIFFERENCES

Category	Spiritual Guidance	Intercessory Prayer	Pastoral Counseling	Counseling Therapy
Goal	Developing and deepening union with God and others	Healing through prayer and sharing	Integration—Healing through Sharing, God as a third member	Healing through identifying needs, values, goals
Immediate Objective	Facilitating prayer and contemplation	Helping an individual move from an extrinsic faith to an intrinsic faith		Helping a person to "cope with life"
Stage 1	Listening - Basic Empathy - Genuineness - Respect - Self-exploration			
Stage II	Advanced Empathy - Self-understanding - Confrontation - Immediacy			
	Identify the Lord in one's life; some possible aspects clarified and known	Sharing and Prayer	Sees life in relation to faith symbols	Focus on the self
Stage III (Action)	Facilitate freedom for the Spirit's movements	Prayer (Speaking at times)	Hope as a virtue	Assess, evaluate, plan, implement, take responsibility
Role of Helper	Secondary to Spirit	with God	Helper more active, role in Church	Patient-Therapist Client-Counselor
Area of Concern	Relation with the Lord, self, and with others	Relationship is restored with God, self, others	Relation with self, God, others	Relation with self, others (the "other")
Relationship with the Helper	to promote and preserve integrity and freedom of an individual's on-going relationship with the Lord	to promote and preserve integrity and freedom of an individual's on-		to promote a relationship with the professional helper in order to promote and facilitate change